Church Is Who We Are

"*Church Is Who We Are* is a systematic, relevant, and biblical exposé of the church that every Christian should embrace."

—Pat P. Glasgow, former president, West Indies School of Theology

"*Church Is Who We Are* is a well-crafted work of literature which supplies the reader with a reservoir of information which can easily serve to form a foundational structure for study in the fundamental nature of the church. I highly recommend this book as a point of reference for a balanced and unbiased view of the church's operation as the redemptive force it was designed to be and a representative of God's government on earth."

—Selwyn Brathwaite, presiding bishop, Barbados District, Pentecostal Assemblies of the West Indies

"Having pastored for more than three decades, I am convinced that this book is a must-read for pastors and leaders, as well as all believers who desire to have a balanced perspective on who we are as the church on earth. Gerald Seale has revealed in this book tremendous insights into the truth about the universal body of Christ and succeeds in making clear what is the nature and purpose of the church."

—Wesley Dear, founder and senior pastor, Covenant Life Teaching Centre

"This is a powerful masterpiece that examines the church from so many angles and aspects, from its birth in the book of Acts down through the centuries, through its development to what we have today. Read and be enlightened. May this transformative message quicken your hearts as the living organism, members of the church on earth."

—Patrick Paul, former general superintendent, Assemblies of God in the Bahamas

"The reader will find at their fingertips an open and honest deep dive into what is church. This book has, and is, causing me to prayerfully examine church the organism and church the organization as well as myself. I sincerely recommend this as a read for church leaders and members as Uncle Gerry, as he is widely known in Barbados, candidly admits the average member is focused on activities; yet in his probative style we come away with a challenge as to who the church is to be."

—Kevin Hunte, pastor, Abundant Life Assembly

Church Is Who We Are

GERALD SEALE

WIPF & STOCK · Eugene, Oregon

CHURCH IS WHO WE ARE

Copyright © 2024 Gerald Seale. All rights reserved. Except for brief quotations in critical publications or reviews, no part of this book may be reproduced in any manner without prior written permission from the publisher. Write: Permissions, Wipf and Stock Publishers, 199 W. 8th Ave., Suite 3, Eugene, OR 97401.

Wipf & Stock
An Imprint of Wipf and Stock Publishers
199 W. 8th Ave., Suite 3
Eugene, OR 97401

www.wipfandstock.com

PAPERBACK ISBN: 979-8-3852-2618-4
HARDCOVER ISBN: 979-8-3852-2619-1
EBOOK ISBN: 979-8-3852-2620-7

Scripture verses, unless otherwise stated, are taken from the New Living Translation, Copyright © 1996, 2004, 2015 by Tyndale House Foundation. Used by permission of Tyndale House Publishers, Inc., Carol Stream, Illinois 60188. All rights reserved.

Scripture verses identified as NIV are taken from The Holy Bible, New International Version® NIV® Copyright © 1973, 1978, 1984, 2011 by Biblica, Inc. Used with permission. All rights reserved worldwide.

Scripture verses identified as NKJV are taken from the New King James Version. Copyright © 1982 by Thomas Nelson, Inc. Used by permission. All rights reserved.

Scripture verses identified as TLV are taken from the Holy Scriptures, Tree of Life Version. © 2014, 2016 by the Tree of Life Bible Society. Used by permission of the Tree of Life Bible Society.

Contents

Chapter 1 – Open to God 1

Chapter 2 – Enigma That Is Church 3

Chapter 3 – Defining Church 14

Chapter 4 – Church Assembled, Church Distributed 36

Chapter 5 – Changing the Way We Think 46

Chapter 6 – Character Reconstruction 51

Chapter 7 – Called to Be Servants 58

Chapter 8 – A Royal Priesthood 64

Chapter 9 – Holy Nation 79

Chapter 10 – Lifestyle Generosity 85

Chapter 11 – Empowered 92

Chapter 12 – Grace-Gift-Person 104

Chapter 13 – Powerfully Indwelled 112

Epilogue 117

Bibliography 119

CHAPTER 1

Open to God

Writing this book has been a challenge. After years of study, the COVID-19 pandemic turned everything upside down. Questions began to be asked about how the Church would emerge after being cocooned away for many months. How would the Church survive without its buildings? What would the Church look like? Should the Church just return to the norms that existed before 2020? Or was God speaking through the pandemic, adjusting the Church for a new era of ministry in a world that had significantly changed in the first two decades of the twenty-first century?

Throughout this book, the term "the Church" is used to mean the global body of people that makes up the Church, irrespective of denominational structures and the schisms that have seemingly torn the visible Church apart. When referring to local congregations, the word "church" is used.

While the question "whither the Church" is important, this book will not attempt to answer that question. Simply, congregations in different cultures will answer the question differently and even congregations within the same culture may have different answers, because God has raised up local congregations to fulfill different purposes under his sovereign direction. This is a season for listening to the voice of God expressed through the Scriptures for the times in which we live.

This book seeks to grapple with the Church as an organism, a living structure of people filled with the Holy Spirit, rather than as an institution. Institution is vital, as pointed out in the next chapter, and serves a critical purpose, but when organism is subsumed under organization, we are in danger of producing a legalistic mechanism that fails to carry out God's agenda in its generation. Organism and organization are both needed for the Church to minister and function effectively in the twenty-first century, and the balance between the two is critical.

How will concepts of organism impact how we think about and practice church? Will we need to change our perspectives and paradigms? Will it mean a radical change in our concept of ministry, what ministry is, and how it is carried out?

Concepts in this book will shake perceptions and will inevitably provoke discussion, even controversy. Yet we must grapple with concepts of Church as organism and how these fit and operate with perceptions of Church as organization. Will our concepts of pastoral roles need to change? Will our opinions on what is ministry and where it is carried out be challenged?

Researching all of this has been revolutionary as the understanding of Church as organism has been sought out in the Christian Scriptures and compared to the realities of the twenty-first century. Christianity can once again revolutionize the world in which we live if we are willing to change some long-held opinions and traditions and allow the organism to flourish within, through, and alongside the organization.

All examples in this book are either taken directly from Scripture or are actual events. Where advisable a few names have been changed to avoid any embarrassment to the people portrayed in the examples.

Enter this book with a heart open to God. Different sections will impact different people because individual Christians and congregations are in different stages of this spiritual journey in Christ through the Holy Spirit. Remaining open to God allows him to guide in the application of these truths in life and ministry.

CHAPTER 2

Enigma That Is Church

THE CHURCH IS REALLY something of an enigma. The Church is clearly a tangible organization but is also a spiritual organism. The Church is local and at the same time universal. The Church is very visible yet undeniably invisible. The Church is one, unified in the purpose of God, and is as diverse as the whole of creation. The Church is divine and yet very human.

ORGANISM AND ORGANIZATION

The Church was birthed as a spiritual organism with the outpouring of the Holy Spirit on the day of Pentecost, which was the full realization of when Jesus breathed on the disciples and said, "Receive the Holy Spirit." What a moment that must have been, the sound of a rushing, mighty wind, something looking like fire above each person's head, and each of the 120 persons speaking a language he or she had not learned (Acts 2:1–4). That spiritual organism, carried in human vessels, spilled onto the streets of Jerusalem and into the temple precincts. Before the day was over, three thousand more had been added to the fledgling Church.

The organism aspect of the Church is inextricably linked with God the Holy Spirit and the spiritual reality of being connected in Jesus Christ through his atoning death on the cross.

There are different ways of expressing belief in the central role of the Holy Spirit in the Christian's life. For some, the Holy Spirit is received through the laying on of hands by the bishop in the sacrament of confirmation. For others, the Holy Spirit is received in a second work of grace as entire sanctification or as the baptism in the Holy Spirit. Still others proclaim that the Holy Spirit makes the sinner alive to God in the new birth experience and no further work of the Holy Spirit is necessary. However, there is firm agreement that God the Holy Spirit is central to the spiritual organism that is Church, and without him the Church is lifeless and impotent.

That spiritual life is tangibly expressed in the book of Acts, which records the history of the first few years of the Church. The pulsating life of this new spiritual organism fills every page of the New Testament book of Acts. The young Church throbs with spiritual life and power demonstrated in incontrovertible ways—the lame walk (Acts 3:7–9, 14:8–11), persons imprisoned are miraculously released (12:1–10), the dead are raised (20:9–12), and demons are cast out (16:16–18), to name just some of the amazing work of the Holy Spirit through God's emerging Church.

As the young Church grew phenomenally in the early days, it did not take long for the apostles to recognize that this spiritual organism that throbbed with the presence and power of the Holy Spirit needed critical organizational elements. Acts 2:41–46 gives a clear indication that from the beginning there was evidence of some measure of deliberate organization. Areas that have contributed specifically to the organization expressed as Church include membership, governance, and discipline.

In Acts 6 that organization was expressed with the appointment of deacons to serve the daily meals. The early organizational aspects can also be seen in the apostle Paul's appointment of leadership in the cities where congregations were formed because of his ministry. It is also seen in the summoning of the first major Church conference in Jerusalem (Acts 15:6–29). It appears in Paul's epistle to Titus, "For this reason I left you in Crete, that you should set in order the things that are lacking and appoint elders in every city as I instructed you" (Titus 1:5). In those early years of local church growth in the first century, the organizational aspect of the Church seems dynamic and far from the static reality which we often now encounter in the twenty-first century.

Down through the centuries the organizational side strengthened as the Church grew. Hierarchies developed for governance and to ensure succession. Strategies were put in place for the management of resources. Procedures and policies were hammered out to handle the problems and resolve the disputes that inevitably arise. The Church could not have developed without proper attention to the organizational dynamics.

Chafer categorically states that the study of ecclesiology cannot advance without the Church as organism being clearly differentiated from the Church as organization. He then shows how some passages of Scripture are best interpreted when the Church is viewed as organism (e.g., Eph 5:25–27) and others when the Church is viewed as organization (Acts 6:1–7).[1]

Denominationalism has accentuated organization to the extent that it seems, at times, as though the organizational and institutional characteristics of the Church have stifled the spiritual organism that is Church with far more theological reflection seemingly given to the Church as organization and institution rather than as organism. When organization becomes an end, the Church atrophies and loses its significance and impact in society.

The term "parachurch" amplifies the concept of Church as institution with another organization coming alongside the institution of Church to assist it in fulfilling its ministry. However, if the people are the Church, then there cannot be a parachurch agency. It is, in fact, the Church in action, the people of God carrying out the purpose of God in this generation. If the people are the Church, wherever the people function, the Church is at work.

The Church needs both competent organizational attention and powerful spiritual life. Both facets are critical to the health and effectiveness of the Church. Berkhof is succinct when he states that the Church as an organism is expressed through all kinds of

---

1. Chafer, *Systematic Theology*, 4:144.

gifts and talents demonstrated and used in its work.[2] However, the Church as institution functions through the structure God has instituted.

For the organism to flourish without continual confusion, it must have organization and structure. Without the reality of the thriving spiritual life of a strong organism, the organization becomes cold, lifeless, without meaning, and nominal in a world desperate for intimacy with the living God. The organization must serve the organism and not vice versa.

LOCAL AND GLOBAL

The Church was born in a local setting with just 120 people in the upper room. Yet even before its birth, the Church was given a global mandate when Jesus said to those gathered on the Mount of Olives just prior to his ascension, "You shall receive power when the Holy Spirit has come upon you; and you shall be witnesses to me in Jerusalem, and in all Judea and Samaria, and to the end of the earth" (Acts 1:8 NKJV). Jesus also emphatically stated the global mandate when he said to the disciples, while in Galilee, between the resurrection and the ascension, "Therefore, go and make disciples of all the nations" (Matt 28:18).

The local congregation is perhaps that part of the Church with which people are most familiar. It is primarily through the local congregation that the Church delivers its multifaceted ministry to the world. The cumulative ministry delivered globally in this way is breathtaking: schools, hospitals, hospices, orphanages, food and agricultural programs, HIV intervention, clean water provision, drug rehabilitation, justice interventions, and the list could go on. The local congregation is an integral part of God's plan for making disciples and expressing his love and compassion to a needy world.

Defining the Church, it can be pointed out that while a specific congregation represents the total Church, there is the enigma that it also embodies locally the totality of all that is Church globally.

---

2. Berkhof, *Systematic Theology*, 567.

This global Church comprises every Christian of every age and we shall finally see them all assembled when Jesus Christ returns as the conquering Messiah, King of kings, and Lord of lords.

The global mandate received increasing attention as we transitioned into the third millennium. The AD 2000 and Beyond Movement was one of the agencies that helped focus attention on the scope of the unfinished task in the final decade of the twentieth century. This has renewed the thrust to have the Bible translated into every spoken language, to develop Christian radio broadcasts in every language, and to see a church planting movement initiated among every people group.

That global mandate has been the inspiration for significant historical movements. With Spain emerging from a centuries-long battle with Muslim invaders, Christopher Columbus was able to garner support for his journey to the "new world." It is known that Columbus sailed, in part, as a religious quest. His voyages were partly intense religious missions. He saw them as the fulfillment of a divine plan for his life and for what he perceived to be the soon-coming end of the world.

David Livingstone, one of the foremost explorers of the nineteenth century, entered Africa to take commerce, Christianity, and civilization, known as Livingstone's three C's, to that continent.[3] Pakenham adds that Livingstone was a philanthropist and quotes Livingstone's December 1857 address to Cambridge University when he said that he was returning to Africa to try to make an open path for commerce and Christianity.[4]

Looking back from the twenty-first century, many Christians would today question if Columbus and Livingstone were really motivated by the worldwide mandate from Jesus. The unequivocal answer is yes. With the benefit of historical hindsight, we can see some of the dreadful, negative consequences on three continents that resulted from the work of these two men. However, available evidence strongly suggests they were both, at least partly, motivated

---

3. Packenham, *Scramble for Africa*, xiii.
4. Packenham, *Scramble for Africa*, 2.

by the Church's global mandate and definitively changed the world they lived in.

William Carey became convinced that the global mandate was incumbent on every Christian. When he first raised it at a ministers' meeting, he was told to sit down as when God wanted to convert the heathen he would do it without human intervention. Carey persisted and when he died in 1834, at age seventy-three, he had been instrumental in the Bible being translated into forty Indian languages, founding a college at Serampore, India, and working to outlaw the burning of widows on the funeral pyres of their dead husbands.

The global dynamic of the Church stretches across space and time embracing some two thousand years of expression in human society.

These contrasting local and global elements can be summed up when it is understood that while the Church is universal in nature, it finds expression in local groups of Christians which display the same qualities as does the body of Christ as a whole. Without both a strong local context and a healthy response to the global mandate, the Church stagnates and shrivels into irrelevancy.

VISIBLE AND INVISIBLE

The Church is highly visible in many countries through its cathedrals, extensive campuses, humble chapels, schools, hospitals, orphanages, senior citizens homes, radio and television programming, food and water distribution, and pervasive ministries that cumulatively impact almost every facet of life.

Yet the Church is invisible in some countries today where Christians are forced to worship in secret because of severe persecution. It is also invisible in the sense that the Lord alone knows who are his (2 Tim 2:19) and only he can separate the genuine wheat from the weeds that make up what is visible to the human eye (Matt 13:24–30). Through this parable of the wheat and the tares, Jesus is extremely specific in teaching that the two are to be allowed to grow together. It is at the ingathering of the harvest that the separation is to be made. We can conclude from the parable that all that is visible is not truly the Church.

This is reinforced by Jesus when he explained to his disciples, "Not everyone who says to Me, 'Lord, Lord,' shall enter the kingdom of heaven, but he who does the will of My Father in heaven. Many will say to Me in that day, 'Lord, Lord, have we not prophesied in Your name, cast out demons in Your name, and done many wonders in Your name?' And then I will declare to them, 'I never knew you; depart from Me, you who practice lawlessness!'" (Matt 7:21–23 NIV). It is possible to profess faith in Christ but never really encounter him as Savior. Similarly, it is entirely possible to be a member of the visible Church and never be part of the invisible Church.

The reformers of the fifteenth and sixteenth centuries saw the aspect of the invisible Church as clearly denunciating that Christ was the sole head of the Church with no human being able to claim such a position. This invisible aspect of the Church is essentially spiritual in nature and the organism still thrives where the organization has been stifled by governmental authorities.

UNITY AND DIVERSITY

That the Church is diverse is unquestionable. When all that makes up Christendom globally is combined, there is a rich mosaic of cultures and practices that characterize the Church in the twenty-first century. These range from the formal and ritualistic through the whole spectrum to the unconventional and seemingly disorganized. Since God has demonstrated his diversity in creation and so many other ways, he clearly accepts, even celebrates, this diversity. Paul acknowledges that diversity in the Church in 1 Cor 12:12–19 using the imagery of the human body.

The same passage goes further to emphasize the unity in Christ that exists amid this diversity (1 Cor 12:20–27). Paul's teaching is that unity does not mean uniformity but is an expression of the global connectedness the Church has as one spiritual organism. Ephesians 4:3–6 explains that this organism has seven points of connectivity—one body, one Spirit, one hope, one Lord, one faith, one baptism, and one God and Father. That connection exists between those who are his, and Paul urges the Christians to make every effort to "keep the unity," not create it. The Church's task is to value and preserve the unity that God has established. Keeping that unity rests on our "lowliness and gentleness, with long-suffering, bearing with one another in love" (Eph 3:2 NKJV). This is, in turn, tied to walking worthy of our calling as Jesus' disciples (Eph 4:1).

Even the uniquely Christian doctrine of the Trinity expresses the concept of unity in diversity, one God (Deut 6:4), but also Father, Son, and Holy Spirit (Matt 3:16–17). So, too, does the understanding that humans are made up of body, soul, and spirit. If this is reduced to just body and spirit, the concept of unity in diversity is still reinforced. The New Testament imagery of the Church as body (Eph 1:22–23; Col 1:18; 2:19), bride (Eph 5:31–32), building (1 Cor 3:9–17), flock (John 10:16, 27), and vine (John 15) inherently convey that concept of unity in diversity.

The same concept is evident in the imagery that Jesus uses of his disciples as a city (Matt 5:14), a field of crops (Matt 13:24), and a group of wedding guests (Mark 2:19). It is, therefore, abundantly clear that when Scripture speaks of the unity of the Church it does not mean uniformity. The Church is not just a collection of individuals; it is a community with genuine unity in very real diversity. Indeed, it can be argued that true Christian unity exists only in diversity. When unity exists outside of diversity there can only be uniformity, and uniformity will, ultimately, begin to erode the life of the organism and guide the Church into dry legalism.

On the night of his betrayal and arrest, Jesus spent time praying in the Garden of Gethsemane on the Mount of Olives. Luke records it was a time of agonizing and earnest prayer (Luke 22:44). John details at least some of that prayer. The things that Jesus prayed about that night must have been a priority in his mind and heart. That should make them a priority for every Christian. In part, Jesus prayed,

> I do not pray for these alone, but also for those who will believe in me through their word; that they all may be one, as you, Father, are in me, and I in you; that they also may be one in us, that the world may believe that you sent me. And the glory which you gave me I have given them, that they may be one just as we are one: I in them, and you in me; that they may be made perfect in one, and that the world may know that you have sent me and have loved them as you have loved me. (John 17:20–23 NIV)

Nothing could more forcefully emphasize the essential unity of Christ's body, the Church.

In an age when the melanin in the human skin seems to divide the body of Christ, we need to be reminded of the essential unity when Scripture declares, "In this new life, it doesn't matter if you are a Jew or a Gentile, circumcised or uncircumcised, barbaric, uncivilized, slave, or free. Christ is all that matters, and he lives in all of us" (Col 3:11).

The Church seems currently to celebrate its diversity and do its best to minimize its oneness. In fact, there is visible evidence that we value our differences far more than we value biblical expressions of unity. Ecumenism is misunderstood and distorted. Individualism and diversity are seemingly celebrated. Rather than maintaining the unity, it almost seems that we actively work to destroy it through suspicion and misrepresentation of each other. Too frequently, personality clashes and bitter disputes over nonessentials disrupt the oneness of the body. In fact, Klyne Snodgrass has pointed out that, regretfully, unity does not exist "between groups, within groups, or even in local congregations."[5]

This emphasizes the Church's disobedience in failing to embrace lowliness, gentleness, long-suffering, and love. Jesus emphatically stated the identifying characteristic of the true Christian, "Your love for one another will prove to the world that you are my disciples" (John 13:35). There is no reasonable excuse for ignoring the clear biblical injunction to unity in all our diversity.

---

5. Snodgrass, *Ephesians*, 210.

As David wrote in Ps 119:63, "I am a friend to anyone who fears you, anyone who obeys your commandments." Are we?

Do we then discard and ignore our differences? No! The biblical reality is unity in diversity, not uniformity. The differences are real. They can be challenging. Our differences can, and often do, disrupt our relationships. In Acts 15 there is a brief record of the first Church council held in Jerusalem. There is a clear intimation that it was, at times, a contentious meeting (Acts 15:2, 7), but the Church worked through the issues and arrived at a clear position together.

Our unity is always in Christ and the Holy Spirit, amid all our diversity. In fact, the beauty of our diversity is celebrated in our unity, and it is only in accepting our diversity that we can experience genuine unity. This is perhaps the hardest part of the Church's enigma to live out in the reality of imperfect humans reflecting the glory of God in unfinished vessels. The constant repetition of the word "same" in 1 Cor 12:4–11 emphasizes the concept of intense unity in genuine diversity. Once again, note that Paul shares what was, for his time, a unique concept of unity in diversity when he declares, "There is no longer Jew or Gentile, slave or free, male and female. For you are all one in Christ Jesus" (Gal 3:28).

Essentially, our unity comes from within. It is a matter of the heart in communion with God, understanding and embracing his purpose for his Church.

DIVINE AND HUMAN

The Church is divine in its origin. It was initiated by Jesus, the second person in the Trinity (Matt 16:18), and fully birthed by the Holy Spirit on the Day of Pentecost in Jerusalem in AD 33 (Acts 2:1–41). Yet the Church is made up entirely of human beings with all their foibles and failings, triumphs and successes. So, the divine infuses the human and the Church bears the visible marks of both.

It has been said for many years that should we find a perfect church or congregation we should not join because the very act of our joining makes that church imperfect.

CONCLUSION

Throughout church history the Church's leaders have struggled to find the balance between these contrasting characteristics. Sometimes we have gotten the dynamics wrong, emphasizing certain aspects to the detriment of others. However, the Holy Spirit has constantly worked within the Church to restore this balance. Where the dynamic tensions are balanced, embraced, and lived out, the Church pulsates with meaning and life-transforming power. Where imbalance predominates, the Church inevitably becomes spiritually cold and lacks the energizing life necessary for effective ministry to the world.

Local and global, organization and organism, visible and invisible, unified and diverse, divine and human, this is the Church that envelops the world and proclaims God's love to all who would respond.

CHAPTER 3

Defining Church

THE MEANING OF THE word "church" has been stretched through the centuries, and today the word has developed a variety of meanings. The word can mean a building in a specific geographical location where people gather for a time of Christian worship. Another common use of the word refers to an order of service or program schedule as in, "Church is held on Sunday mornings at 9:00 a.m." The word can also mean a denomination, an institution. This was not the essential essence of what Jesus had in mind when he stated, "I will build my church" (Matt 16:18).

Many of our congregations are caught up in the endless activity on Sunday morning, Sunday night, Tuesday night, and Friday night (even during and post-COVID), a cycle of activity that has become an end in itself with no visible productivity, no measurable outcome beyond the number of attendees, and the size of the offerings received. Program is useful as it can provide the means through which the Church can function and by which the members are able to constructively engage the world in which we live and minister. However, when the program becomes an end in itself, we have lost the true essence of Church and are in very serious danger of building personal kingdoms rather than the kingdom of God.

Like the word "synagogue," the word "church" began as a reference to the people who gathered to worship and, in the process of time, morphed into meaning the building in which they worshiped. Through the two millennia of its existence, the term has also been impregnated with the concepts of institution, as discussed in the previous chapter.

Proper organization is essential. Aspects of institutionalization are necessary and helpful. However, if, in the end, all we have is an institution, a building, and a program, then the Church has essentially been rendered lifeless and ineffective. It was not Jesus' intention that the Church would be an end in itself, but it is intended to be a tool in the providence of God to initiate transformation in individuals and societies all across the world.

In looking at the organism side of the Church, it can be defined as a universal community of people in blood covenant with God by faith, imbued with the Holy Spirit, and being discipled to be radically different, impacting the society in which they live.

It is time to recapture the concept of *people* being the Church and reinvigorate the organism, pulsating with the presence and power of the Holy Spirit.

UNIVERSAL COMMUNITY

Christians are expected to be in a personal relationship with the Triune God. However, the Church is also a community of people, not just an isolated individual. Too often these two aspects of the Church, individual relationship and community, have been presented in opposition to each other when they are both a critical part of the enigma that is Church. We need both the individual's walk with God and the relationships within the community of the redeemed. Indeed, the full extent of the Church as community embraces a community of faith, of compassion, of the Holy Spirit, and of evangelism.

There is only one Church. There are thousands of denominations and millions of congregations, but only one Church. If the Church is Jesus' bride and he is monogamous, then he is coming for one bride. While this concept of one Church is readily accepted mentally by most Christians, it is challenging to work out the practical reality of this in a meaningful way. If we believe one thing and live out the opposite isn't that the very definition of hypocrisy?

Boice has correctly pointed out that the Church is the complete grouping of those who follow Christ.[1] Thiessen reinforces this concept of one community when he reminds us that the Church consists of all those who have experienced the new birth of the Holy Spirit and have, by that same Spirit, been placed in the body of Christ.[2] Dusing reiterates that the biblical meaning of the word "church" refers primarily to people who have come to a saving knowledge of Christ and not to institutions or structures.[3]

If the Church is really one community of people, we may need to rethink what we're doing. Yes, there are important institutional and organizational aspects to the Church. However, the essence of the Church is not the hierarchy, the buildings, the bylaws, the protocols and policies, or the political power plays. The fundamental nature of the Church is the community of people and everything else is but a tool to serve the people and empower them to be the agents of change in a world seemingly doing its best to forget God.

It is the Greek word *ekklesia* that is translated "church" in the Bible. It was a commonly used word in New Testament times referring to an assembly of people. Outside of Scripture it had a political rather than a religious connotation. The best understanding of the word would seem to be a "coming together" or an "assembly of people."

Ryrie taught that in the biblical meaning of the Greek word, as used in the New Testament, there is a much deeper meaning as the people themselves, whether assembled or distributed through society, are the *ekklesia*.[4] Guthrie concludes that *ekklesia* in Scripture is a group of people belonging to God and not an organization or institution.[5] Indeed, the centrality in the Christian Scriptures of the community idea cannot be overemphasized.

1. Boice, *Ephesians*, 126–28.
2. Thiessen, *Lectures in Systematic Theology*, 311.
3. Dusing, "New Testament Church," 526.
4. Ryrie, *Basic Theology*, 456.
5. Guthrie, *New Testament Theology*, 712.

Although salvation is applied individually, and the processes of Holy Spirit empowerment and sanctification must be personally pursued, there is no sense in which the New Testament conceives of lone believers. The repeated emphasis on groups of believers shows the basic character of the scriptural idea of the Church.

Have evangelical Christians so emphasized the personal relationship with God that we have forgotten the biblical reality of God in community? We cannot back away from the incredible significance of the individual's relationship with God. This is vital to each person's salvation and entrance into the new covenant of salvation. However, we can so personalize and privatize God that we forget the equally important biblical concept of God present in and working through the community of believers. The Church is not an individual. Jesus set the standard as being "two or three" at the very least (Matt 18:20). The Church is a community of believers. No other definition will suffice to meet the criteria of God's word to us.

Throughout the New Testament, the Church is shown in a context of community, whether, for example, as meeting in a specific home or as a group of believers in a city. While salvation is accepted individually and there are many injunctions to personal holiness, the Bible does not seem to conceive of independent believers living and functioning completely on their own. Rather, the injunction is emphatic, "Let us consider one another in order to stir up love and good works, not forsaking the assembling of ourselves together, as is the manner of some" (Heb 10:24–25 NKJV). Jesus reinforced the concept of community when he stated that he would be present "where two or three are gathered together in My name" (Matt 18:20).

Soungalo reminds us that the nature and value of the ties that bind Christians with each other should be stronger than any other kinship.[6] What is born of the Spirit is of more value than what is born of the flesh (Matt 10:35–37; 12:46–50; John 3:1–21). So, the Bible calls all believers to strong community life.

---

6. See Soungalo, "Family," 1174.

It is important to recognize that a community is more than just a collection of people. Community implies meaningful relationships where people share common perspectives, accountability, celebration, and encouragement; express love, acceptance, forgiveness, and spirituality; and share a sense of purpose and vision.

The Christian concept of fellowship adds to the perspective of Church as community. Christian fellowship is first rooted in the Christian's relationship with the Father, Son, and Holy Spirit. Out of the fellowship of that divine-human relationship develops the spiritual fellowship believers share within the community of the Church. "If the goal of discipleship is to become Christ-like, it's important that we spend time with others, learning how to love and be loved and letting our rough edges be sanded away."[7] Acts 2:42–47 extended the concept of fellowship to the sharing of material possessions, which is reinforced in Paul's epistles (e.g., 2 Cor 8 and 9).

Sometimes Christians substitute the word "communion" for "fellowship," though "communion" has, in some sectors of the Church, become, increasingly, used exclusively of the sharing of bread and wine in remembrance of the crucifixion of Christ. In some parts of the Church "fellowship" has been reduced to simply getting together for food. It is important that we recapture the depths of the richness of Christian fellowship that is spiritual and material.

The Christian concept of fellowship is impregnated with the interaction between God and humans that enriches the consequent relationship between humans so that the community of believers is enriched spiritually, materially, emotionally, socially, intellectually, and psychologically.

So then, the Church is a community of believers in fellowship with the Triune God and with each other at the local and global levels. Scripture does not at any time conceive of isolated believers existing entirely outside the general body of believers known as the

---

7. Spangler and Tverberg, *Sitting at the Feet*, 72.

Church. Christianity is about relationships with the Trinity and each other that transform lifestyles.

Among the challenges to our unity in Christ are three valuable principles embraced by congregations across the world. These include that congregations should be self-governing, self-supporting, and self-propagating. While these principles can and do help congregations to grow and develop, the unintended consequence is a strong self-sufficiency leading to the erroneous belief that the congregation does not need anyone or anything outside itself. This belief flies in the face of the community concepts in Scripture. Can we embrace the good of these principles while being aware of the negative challenges of intense self-sufficiency so that the Church begins moving back to the sense of communal, national, and global interdependence?

The incredible significance of the individual's relationship with God cannot be relegated to the sidelines. This is vital to each person's salvation and entrance into the covenant. However, God can be so personalized and privatized that the equally important biblical concept of God present in, and working through, the community of believers is forgotten. The Church is not an individual. The Church is a community of believers. No other definition will suffice to meet the criteria of God's word to us.

If the community of people is brought back to the center of our concept of the Church, then the Church, as currently expressed in many countries, must change. The Church does not exist to serve its cardinals, bishops, apostles, prophets, and institutions. Rather, these persons exist to serve the Church, the people, and empower these people to change society.

The *Midweek Nation* newspaper in Barbados on August 18, 2020, made this comment in its editorial, "By the church we refer not to the hundreds of structures, some more Gothic and grand than others, that dot the landscape from St. Lucy in the north to Christ Church in the south, but to the ordinary men and women who regularly congregate to worship their God, practice their faith and profess their Christian virtues."[8] It is time that these "ordinary

---

8. See editorial, *Midweek Nation*, August 18, 2020, 8.

men and women" be fully equipped to take their vocations and professions into society on the bedrock of Christian principles, precepts, and promises.

Once we define Church as a community of people, we need to enable and empower these people to function as Church (salt and light) in society. We have too often restricted Church to Sunday morning at a specific time, in a specific location, with a specific program or order of service. Yet if Church is people, then Church is Church twenty-four hours a day, seven days a week. Church remains Church every morning, but we have been conditioned by our mindset to equip the Church to function when it is gathered on Sunday morning and have not equipped it to function as Church all the other days of the week.

Considering all that is happening globally, can the Church be equipped to function as the Church twenty-four hours a day, seven days a week when distributed through the community and not only when gathered in a building?

The Church is seemingly in love with the inside of its buildings while this post-modern generation longs to see a practical demonstration of the reality of Christ outside on the street and throughout society. We must balance public proclamation of the "good news" with incarnation of that "good news" in the communities where Christians live. While the truth that salvation is the gift of God and not of works is widely understood, many are yet to grasp the biblical reality that "we are God's masterpiece. He has created us anew in Christ Jesus, so we can do the good things he planned for us long ago" (Eph 2:10). The people must be equipped and released to do good works in the world that the world might see the glory of God and that his glory might fill the earth like the waters cover the sea.

It is urgent that the Church's leaders move outside the box in which they think and plan. These boxes were developed during a time and by conditions that have changed significantly. The boxes were not wrong in the time they were developed. Now we need to step outside of these boxes and ask the Holy Spirit to empower thinking in terms of contemporary situations so that the Church's message remains relevant. As the shepherd David stepped out of the box of the conventional military strategies of his time when he accepted Goliath's challenge to single combat, so the Church must step out of those boxes fashioned in the twentieth century when the world was radically different from what it is now.

As we move outside the "think-box" we have been given by those who have gone before, we will see brand new opportunities for ministry that will significantly impact the society in which we minister. We must remain constantly open to God and allow him to show us new openings and unusual opportunities.

The Church must provide apostolic leadership within the community. This is not just conferring the title "apostle" on a few leaders within the Church gathered, but equipping the Church distributed to take apostolic ministry throughout the society to the marketplace, the school, the village, the corporate boardroom, etc. Blood-bought, Spirit-filled, sold-out disciples must be equipped to go make a difference.

The Church must be a prophetic voice in the community. Again, this is not just a few leaders within the Church gathered speaking to national issues. This is the Church distributed, empowered to speak into every committee on which they serve, every business or social meeting in which they participate, in their schools, and workplaces, anointed by the Holy Spirit to speak into their situations with the power of God to see change.

The Church as a living organism penetrates every area of society in which it ministers. That penetration carries salt and light into every corner of the Caribbean and the world, to every valley and mountain, every village and town. Can that reality be maximized to see powerful changes, or will the Church remain cloistered in its buildings, only venturing forth to snatch the occasional soul from the fires of hell?

It is time for the Church to become, once again, people-focused rather than remaining primarily institution-focused.

Could it be that something of the gospel has been missed by moving so far from the concept of God in community? Individuals must be introduced to personal faith in Christ. The importance of restored relationships between individuals and the Father through Jesus must be highly valued. The desire of God to work in community, the community of the Church in covenant with him and through the Church to the community in which the Church exists, must never be forgotten.

BLOOD COVENANT

The people who, together, constitute the Church are in a blood covenant with God by faith. A covenant is an agreement that legally binds and is usually considered unbreakable. In one expression of the blood covenant, each party to the covenant would cut his hand, drip blood into the same cup of wine, stir the wine and blood together, and then each would drink from the same cup. Henry Stanley, the man who sought and found David Livingstone in Africa, recounts participating in such a covenant ritual in Africa that changed his fortunes at the time.[9]

The Christian blood covenant was established by God on the cross of Jesus. Hebrews 9:22 states, "According to the law almost all things are purified with blood, and without shedding of blood there is no remission" (NKJV). Since animal and human blood was insufficient to ensure humankind's total forgiveness, God the Son took human form and poured out his blood to develop the basis of an infinite covenant extended to "whoever believes in him" (John 3:16). Humans can add nothing to the covenant. We accept by faith what God has done as the adequate propitiation for our sins. "For by grace you have been saved through faith, and that not of yourselves; it is the gift of God, not of works, lest anyone should boast" (Eph 2:8–9 NKJV).

In the case of the Christian's blood covenant, the two parties, God and man, are unequal. God provided the blood, and he has made the commitment. Humans, as the lesser partner in the covenant, cannot alter it but can only accept it by faith or reject it altogether. Scripture does not recognize the agnostic who tries

---

9. Handschumacher, "Stanley Covenant," para. 2–4.

to sit on the fence. As Jesus himself said, "Anyone who isn't with me opposes me, and anyone who isn't working with me is actually working against me" (Luke 11:23).

In accepting the new covenant, men and women enter a relationship built on what God has done. The effectiveness of the covenant depends on the infinite worth of the blood of his Son, Jesus Christ. Jesus's blood not only guarantees the covenant but also cleanses from sin so that the believer stands before God as though he had never sinned. This blood will be the basis of the reconciliation to God of everything in creation (Col 1:19–20).

Such a covenant means that God can be depended on to fulfill his promises, abide by his precepts, and work through his principles regardless of the situation. God has bound himself to redeemed humanity by a blood covenant.

The cup also plays a significant part in this covenant as Christians symbolically drink from a cup every time they celebrate the Lord's Supper (Holy Communion) as a potent metaphorical reminder of the blood poured out on Calvary for their salvation and symbolically as the cup of suffering Jesus drank on our behalf.

The Church, then, is a universal community in blood covenant with God.

IMBUED WITH THE HOLY SPIRIT

An individual's salvation is wrought through the power and presence of the Holy Spirit because of the blood of Jesus shed on the cross. It is a divine work of the third Person in the Trinity. That presence and power was integral to the early Church in the first decades and centuries of the Church's existence. This remains critical now, more than twenty centuries later. A subsequent chapter will develop this more fully.

Church Is Who We Are

BEING DISCIPLED TO BE RADICALLY DIFFERENT

The Matt 28 mandate given by Jesus was not just to go and win souls. It was to go and make disciples. Jesus explained what he meant by the term "disciple," "Teaching them to observe all things I have commanded you" (Matt 28:19). In fact, the term "disciple" is the only descriptive word used in the Gospels of the followers of Jesus. In the New Testament the verb is used 25 times and the noun more than 260 times.[10]

During the period when Jesus lived, the term "disciple" was widely used to mean someone who was apprenticed in a trade, the student of a teacher, or committed to studying a specific subject. This is all rich imagery for a Christian disciple as our lives become apprenticed to Christ to learn his way of life. Christians are his students and are committed to specifically studying his teachings for their practical application in their lives and then making that application, so they live out in their lives the rich truths of their Mentor, the Lord Jesus Christ.

Paul captures the essential outcome of discipleship when he tells the church at Ephesus that they are to "all come to such unity in our faith and knowledge of God's Son that we will be mature in the Lord, measuring up to the full and complete standard of Christ" (Eph 4:13 NKJV). That is a comprehensive remake of lifestyle which implies a radical change in worldview. Such a change can only be described as radical because so much must be revolutionized. Paul identifies this by stating the necessity of "changing the way you think" (Rom 12:2). This is a complete change of mindset which necessitates a change of basic worldview. Wiersbe has noted that the transformation is not just religious but also cultural.[11]

When we examine the teaching of Jesus it is immediately apparent that it is radically different from the societal norms, even in the twenty-first century. For example, if struck in the face, the disciple of Jesus turns the other cheek rather than striking back (Matt 6:39). Then there is the principle of "love your enemies! Pray for

---

10. Rabey, *Side by Side*, 33.
11. Wiersbe, *Exposition Commentary*, 1:553–58.

those who persecute you!" (Matt 5:44). That is radically different to the prevailing societal culture in which the Church ministers.

This is an inner revolution that works its way out into lifestyles and interpersonal relationships. Such a revolution is inherent in a personal relationship with Jesus and could be characterized as based on fervent love. This love leads to a willing personal identification with his cross and an ongoing commitment to embrace and practice his teachings. Where there is a strong commitment to his teachings without the passionate love relationship, the outcome can easily be a harsh legalism. Where there is fervent love for him without the corresponding commitment to his teachings, the result easily slips away from the holiness which we first experienced when we came to Jesus. "No, dear brothers and sisters, I have not achieved it, but I focus on this one thing: forgetting the past and looking forward to what lies ahead, I press on to reach the end of the race and receive the heavenly prize for which God, through Christ Jesus, is calling us" (Phil 3:13–14).

The Christian disciple's experience is one of continual growth and shaping as they study the teachings of Scripture and conform their lives to the principles, precepts, and promises found there. The more the disciple studies and applies these truths, the more radical the inner change revealed in the outer lifestyle.

It is impossible to become a genuine disciple of Jesus and not be radically different from the world in which we live. The miracle of being quickened by the Holy Spirit opens a spiritual dimension in our lives that is nothing short of revolutionary. The process of the renewing of the mind (Rom 12:1–2) changes the way one thinks and, once the way one thinks changes, the way one talks and acts changes because the issues of life proceed from the inside out according to Jesus (Matt 15:18–19).

This is not talking about struggling under condemnation to live in accordance with Scripture, though there are struggles Christians must go through as the spiritual revolution works itself out in their lives. This is about the reality of inner change coming through the freshness of the relationship with the Trinity until the life of the Father, Son, and the Holy Spirit transforms on the inside, making people radically different. It is not something done in human strength but something God does, and it is radical! We are not passive in the process, so must daily take the time to build that radicalizing inner relationship with God in Jesus through the Holy Spirit.

Christians are each, individually, at different stages of spiritual development, but there must be ongoing spiritual growth that causes radical change as the purpose of God is pursued in each person's life. In the physical realm, when there is no growth and change there is an indication that death is taking over. This is no less true in the spiritual sphere.

Today, sections of the Church have become offhand with the radical truths of Christianity. This overfamiliarity has caused too many Christians to fail in discerning the far-reaching nature of the things Jesus taught and how they impact every aspect of life.

Too many congregations have growing numbers of "members" who never attend a single service. Even among those who attend, there seems to be little effort to understand, implement, and live out the radical teachings of Jesus. Anecdotal evidence suggests that even daily reading of the Bible is not a norm for many believers.

The disciple, the one who studies the teachings of the master to implement them through his lifestyle, does not become nonchalant in the process, but is constantly molded and renewed by those teachings as they are searched out for understanding and practical, personal application in life.

So much emphasis is currently being laid on motivational sermons, based, in part, on a worldview rooted in contemporary culture, that there is danger of losing the radical nature of discipleship embedded in the mindset of Christ and brought into focus by his cross. There is urgency in the call to return to radical discipleship. It is only in such discipleship that a degenerate world can see the glory of the crucified Christ and it is only the crucified Christ who can revolutionize characters, circumstances, and cultures. To settle for less is to fail to be the Church and to shortchange the people around us who so desperately need the Truth, Christ Jesus.

IMPACTING THE SOCIETY

When the apostle Paul entered Thessalonica, the capital and business center of the Roman province of Macedonia, on his second missionary journey, he spent three Saturdays in discussions with the Jews and gentile "God-fearers" at one of the local synagogues. Paul's strategy was to go to the largest and more important cities first, start in the synagogues, and then use those cities as centers to take the gospel to surrounding towns and villages. Luke records, "Some of the Jews who listened were persuaded and joined Paul and Silas, along with many God-fearing Greek men and quite a few prominent women" (Acts 17:4).

This large number of conversions provoked a violent reaction from the Jews who had rejected Paul's message. Unable to find Paul, they dragged Jason and some of the other Christians before the city's rulers. There, the accusers charged these "who have caused trouble all over the world and now they're disturbing our city too" (Acts 17:6). The thrust of the original Greek translated "caused trouble all over the world" could be rendered "caused a radical social upheaval." This charge made sense in the contemporary situation as the preceding decade had seen turbulence provoked by Jews in various cities in the Roman Empire. While it was intended to be a charge of sedition and possible treason, it remains an incredible charge to be laid against a Christian! The powerful impact of the gospel has not lessened. It still turns lives and communities upside down, or right side up, and generates positive, radical, social upheaval.

While there are numerous stories of the impact of the gospel coming out of the developing world, it seems that the Church is on full retreat in the West. Is it that discipleship has slipped from the preeminent place Jesus gave it? Has the Church in the West fallen into the Laodicean trap?

> You say, "I am rich. I have everything I want. I don't need a thing!" And you don't realize that you are wretched and miserable and poor and blind and naked. So I advise you to buy gold from me, gold that has been purified by fire.

Then you will be rich. Also buy white garments from me so you will not be shamed by your nakedness, and ointment for your eyes so you will be able to see. (Rev 3:17–18)

Is it possible that we have also been so affected by the expectation of the second coming of Jesus that we have lost our ability to impact the present and so change the future? Around 1960, the leaders of a Pentecostal denomination approached the owner of a plantation in St. John, in the Caribbean Island of Barbados, expressing a desire to purchase land on which to erect a church building. The owner readily agreed and offered to sell them any portion of almost three acres of land that was totally unsuitable for agriculture. Because Jesus was expected soon, the Pentecostal leaders selected a few thousand square feet. The owner subsequently donated the balance of the land to the village as a park and the congregation remains in a small building awaiting the return of Jesus.

Has "rapture paralysis" so influenced some parts of the twenty-first century Church in the West that it is incapable of impacting the society in which it exists? Has this led some of Christ's disciples to withdraw from society because Jesus is coming soon anyhow, so what they do in societal transformation won't make a difference anyway? Or is it that Jesus is expected to destroy everything when he returns and build all things new, so we hunker down awaiting his triumphant return? How does this line up against the Matt 28:17–19 and Acts 1:8 mandates given by Jesus? When did the mandate change from making disciples to looking for the rapture and withdrawing from society until he comes?

Has the Church turned inward, causing the outward focus to dim? Have we become so enamored with motivational messages and steps to receiving blessing and prosperity that we are no longer moved with the powerful compassion that thrust out William Booth (founder of the Salvation Army), propelled John Calvin (who changed the "smelliest city in Europe," Geneva, into a garden)[12] or moved Jesus to feed the five thousand (Matt 14:14–21)?

Let us rekindle the impact like that which caused the Right Excellent Samuel Sharpe, an African slave who was a Baptist deacon, to lead a rebellion in Jamaica in late 1831 into early 1832. Convinced that the Bible taught that no man should be enslaved, he sought, initially, by peaceful means and civil disobedience to end the system that oppressed millions of Africans in European colonies across the world. The rebellion of fifty thousand slaves from 160 plantations in Jamaica was put down by the planters and the British army after some months and Sharpe was executed in May 1832.[13] He is now a national hero of Jamaica.

The same month Sharpe was executed, the British House of Commons appointed a committee to examine the needed legislation to end slavery throughout the British Empire. Fourteen months later, a bill to emancipate the slaves was laid before the British Parliament, becoming effective August 1, 1834. It has been suggested that the revolution led by Sharpe reset the agenda of the British Empire and brought the complete abolition of African chattel slavery much quicker than may have otherwise been possible. Of course, Christians such as William Wilberforce, assisted by the Quakers and other committed Christians in England like Granville Sharpe, Thomas Clarkson, James Ramsay, and John Newton, sponsored the legislation and worked from within the British House of Commons to achieve this result. This is a powerful reminder of the gospel that turns established society upside down.

Simeon Nsibambi was another man used by God in a revival that swept East Africa in the mid-twentieth century. In hungering for God Nsibambi, the son of a chief of the Buganda nation in Uganda, deepened his relationship with Jesus and molded his life on God's word, learning and implementing the teachings of Christ in his life. He was deeply impacted by the teaching coming out of the Keswick Convention. Subsequently, Nsibambi became

---

12. Cunningham, *Transforms Nations*, 86–97.
13. Sherlock and Bennett, *Story of the Jamaican People*, 212–28.

the patriarch of a movement that altered East African Christianity, and millions were touched by the revival that represented a vital Christianity which was shaped by African leadership[14] (see further details in the Christian History Magazine, Issue 79, 2003).

The community of Buxton in Guyana has been known for violence and criminal activity. Some years ago, Buxton barricaded itself against the world, blockading the roads entering the community. The national security forces were tentative about entering Buxton and tension began to build in the country. The Georgetown Ministers Association called Christians together to pray and, subsequently, several of them entered Buxton unopposed, mounting and dismantling the barricades, and praying on every street throughout the community. A possible national crisis was defused.

Similarly, the road between Guyana and Brazil was blockaded at a bridge that crosses a river in the town of Linden, bringing commercial activity to a halt. Leaders of the Church in Linden met with the dissenters and were able to persuade them to reopen the bridge and allow normal activity between the two countries to resume. This prompted Bharrat Jagdeo, then president of the Republic of Guyana and a Hindu, to recognize the role the Church can play in national transformation.

Dr. Wonsuk Ma, a Korean who served as vice president for Academic Affairs of the Asia Pacific Theological Seminary (Philippines), in a paper presented at the Global Christian Forum Asia Consultation in 2004, strongly made the point that evangelicals globally have historically empowered the poor and made God someone who is intimately involved in our daily lives.

Down through history the thread of the impact of the devoted disciples of Jesus is clearly discernible. Lives transformed by the gospel and lived out in the community of the redeemed in obedience to the teaching of Jesus impact societies at every level and in every age. Change for the better comes in those societal upheavals, and social revolutions transform communities and nations. Biblical discipleship is inherently transformational, in any culture and at any time.

---

14. Shaw, "Hunger for Holiness."

Christians have altered the course of nations through their lives and actions. As shown above, this societal change can be traced in history.

Around AD 400, Ireland was a pagan nation steeped in slave-trading and idolatry. One man, Patrick, who was born in Great Britain, changed the course of Irish history. He arrived in Ireland in AD 432 and, during some twenty-seven years of ministry, helped plant hundreds of churches and schools, converted some three thousand pagan priests and all the chieftains, and brought an end to slavery in Ireland. He changed a nation in less than one generation. He is remembered now as St. Patrick, and a day is named after him and is celebrated annually across the world, especially by those with Irish ancestry.[15]

It also happened in Scotland when Prince David, the sixth son of King Malcolm, ascended to the throne in 1124 as David I, king of Scots. A godly man—whose mother has been canonized and is now known as St. Margaret; a man who had a brother who was bishop in the Celtic Church, and another brother who was a bishop in the Roman Catholic Church; a man who loved God and has himself been canonized—set out to change Scotland.

On May 24, 1153, when they went to awaken the king of Scots, they found David dead, kneeling beside his bed in the posture of prayer. The king of Scots had passed into his master's presence on his knees. Nigel Tranter, perhaps Scotland's most prolific historical writer of the twentieth century, describes King David as one of Scotland's greatest sons, and records that he left a different nation behind him. Tranter further records that in the almost thirty years David reigned, he had changed Scotland more than any other man before or since.[16]

Abraham Kuyper became prime minister of the Netherlands in 1901. History records the complete change of that country as a Christ-surrendered, Holy Spirit-filled man led the nation into discipleship to Christ. Kuyper passionately believed that there is not

---

15. Arnold, "St. Patrick's Day."
16. Tranter, *Story of Scotland*, 35–45.

a single patch of life over which Christ does not claim complete sovereignty.[17]

Joan Purcell has given her life to serving God as a royal priest in the Parliament of Grenada in the Caribbean She served as a member of cabinet and subsequently as president of the senate in the government of Grenada. It was Purcell, in her capacity as a member of the cabinet at the time, who wrestled in prayer with the decision and finally commuted the death sentences of the persons convicted of murdering former Grenadian Prime Minister Maurice Bishop and other government ministers in a failed coup. She believes (as told to the author in conversation) God guided her decision and, through it, aided the process of healing and reconciliation in Grenada after a period of national tumult. All of those whose death sentences were commuted were said to be hard core communists, but have gone on to lead productive lives, many of them as committed Christians.[18]

Albouystown in Guyana is known as an economically depressed area where violence is more the norm than the exception. Some years ago, Apostle Elsworth Williams accepted the challenge of pastoring a small congregation on Cooper Street, a part of the community nicknamed Hell's Kitchen because of the tangible presence of crime. Undaunted, Williams served God in that community with the anointing of the Holy Spirit. As the congregation grew numerically and spiritually, change began to gradually infiltrate the community until change was so tangible that the nickname Hell's Kitchen was changed to Heaven's Drawing Room. Today the congregation, operating under the name Heavenly Light World Outreach, serves the community with worship, discipleship, a preschool, a counselling center, and several training programs. Growing Christian influence can definitively change society.[19]

For four hundred and eighty years, the economy of The Bahamas was dominated by a small minority of people, strengthened by

---

17. Cunningham, *Transforms Nations*, 51–57.
18. Purcell, *Memoirs*, 119–38.
19. Author's personal visits to Georgetown, Guyana, and conversations with Apostle Elsworth Williams and his son Eworth.

colonial rule at the expense of most people, who were descended from African slaves and who were widely treated as second-class citizens. During the struggle for majority rule, the Church in The Bahamas played a pivotal role in providing platforms for grassroot political leaders who represented the masses. The Church organized prayer meetings and gatherings to encourage and strengthen members to believe in themselves and the power of God to change the social and economic injustices. Prominent clergy in this movement were men like Rev. Dr. H. W. Brown, Rev. Dr. Samuel Colebrooke, and Rev. Dr. R. E. Cooper.

Five years after majority rule was attained, the political influence was for The Bahamas to take another step and determine its own destiny, becoming an independent nation on July 10, 1973. The influence of Christian leaders caused core Christian values to be enshrined into the preamble of the constitution. The idea was that the Church would be a sustaining arm to take the nation to its Christian destiny, and this is reflected in the country's national anthem.[20]

These examples pungently highlight parts of our powerful Christian heritage spanning the centuries.

The Church is intended to impact the society in which it exists. We have tended to look at the Great Commission in Matt 28:19–20 in terms only of the individuals who come to Christ being discipled to be followers of Christ. Christians have focused so heavily on the individual relationship that, seemingly, the corporate relationship that is also clear in Scripture has been overlooked.

When the psalmist wrote in what is considered a messianic psalm, "Only ask, and I will give You the nations as Your inheritance, the whole earth as Your possession" (Ps 2:8), what was included? If each of our nations is included, did Jesus ask for a few citizens, or did he ask for the complete nation? If he asked for the complete nation, does he really want all of it, the people, the economy, the moral fabric of the society, the culture, the political processes and the institutions and structures of the society? Or does he just want a few citizens to populate New Jerusalem?

---

20. Author's personal communications with the Rev. Dr. Patrick Paul.

So what impact is the Church, the entire bride of Christ, having nationally in every country in the world?

It is hard to reconcile the statistic that Jamaica has the highest number of churches per square mile globally and one of the highest murder rates in the world. It is difficult to go to The Bahamas and be told that 44 percent of Bahamians are born again, but they have the same, or higher, crime rate as Barbados, where 25 percent are born again. Or to go to Haiti and be told more than 30 percent of the population is born again, with some of the largest congregations in the Caribbean, yet see the extreme poverty, the violence, and the confusion. It is impossible to reconcile the reality that 70 percent of Barbadians say they go to church, but more than 70 percent of the babies are born outside of wedlock and anecdotal evidence suggests that two or three babies are aborted for every baby born in that island nation!

The more the individuals who make up the community we call Church are changed, the more the impact on society. There are no simple answers. The nature of the societies in which we live is complicated, the variety of circumstances demand so many different responses, and the frailty of humanity in confronting institutionalized evil is real. As Paul said to the saints at Ephesus, "We are not fighting against flesh and blood enemies, but against evil rulers and authorities of the unseen world, against mighty powers in this dark world, and against evil spirits in the heavenly places" (Eph 6:12).

One person submitted to the lordship of Jesus can make a difference. Yet Jesus does not want just the individual. He wants it all.

In using an illustration to describe the kingdom of God, Jesus likened it to yeast. "What else is the Kingdom of God like? It is like the yeast a woman used in making bread. Even though she put only a little yeast in three measures of flour, it permeated every part of the dough" (Luke 13:20–21). The power of a small amount of yeast to change the dough is an image of the power of the Church to impact and change society.

There is a village in Texas with a population of about five hundred. One description of this village is that it has a city limits sign at each end with not a whole lot in between. It would be a tragedy if that should describe the total impact of Christianity on the societies in which we live, move, and have our being.

As the process of discipleship becomes imbedded in the lives of person after person, will not the community where these people live begin to change? When community after community changes through the radically different disciples living within each community, will not the nation begin to change?

In Matt 5:15–16 Jesus equates letting our light shine with doing "good deeds." It is our behavior, rather than our words, that causes God to be glorified. As the apostle Peter points out, "Be careful to live properly among your unbelieving neighbors. Then even if they accuse you of doing wrong, they will see your honorable behavior, and they will give honor to God when he judges the world" (1 Pet 2:12).

The Church does not exist to maintain the status quo. Neither is the Church a completed or fixed entity. It is a dynamic, living organism growing and developing in each generation. The Church exists to foment revolution in lifestyles through biblical discipleship, to challenge the structures of evil in society, to glorify God through deeds, and to build God's kingdom in the hearts of men and women.

When the very essence of the Church is misunderstood and misrepresented, the gospel that the Church preaches becomes distorted and, in some cases, perverted. Indeed, the Church is a universal community of people in blood covenant with God by faith, imbued with the Holy Spirit, and being discipled to be radically different, impacting the society in which they live.

CHAPTER 4

Church Assembled, Church Distributed

WHEN A COMMUNITY OF believers gathers in the name of Jesus Christ for worship and to study the Scriptures, the Church has assembled. Usually this is at least a couple of times a week, and is not dependent on numbers or location. There are other times the Church assembles for programs aimed at specific age groups, to handle its organizational needs, or to address specific issues. The rest of the time, the Church is distributed throughout the community where the people live. However, assembled or distributed, the Church is still the Church.

CHURCH ASSEMBLED

The Church normally assembles to worship or to transact the business of the congregation. Different national and denominational cultures have shaped how this looks around the world. There is wide diversity in worship forms from very structured liturgical formats to what appears to be almost no structure at all. Yet there are certain elements that are common to our various assembled congregations.

The Scriptures are a part of these gatherings. The Bible is publicly read and, usually, there is a time of teaching from it. John

Calvin, the reformer, was adamant that the Church is wherever the Bible is preached and heard. Some denominations have placed the pulpit in the center of the platform at the front of the building to strongly emphasize the primacy of Scripture in their thinking and times of congregational gathering. Proclamation of God's word to his people is always given primacy in this style of corporate worship.

When assembled the Church participates in the ordinances, also called rites or sacraments. These were established within the Church by Jesus and vary in number from two to seven among the denominations. Everyone agrees that, at least, the Lord's Supper (Holy Communion) and water baptism are necessary.

Some gatherings have placed the altar at the center of their platforms to emphasize the importance to them of the sacramental elements in worship. While some denominations believe that the ordinances themselves produce spiritual change, evangelical Christians see them as symbols that represent already existing inner spiritual realities.

Assembling provides the opportunity to edify or strengthen and build up each other. Paul addresses this reality to the congregation that met in Corinth, "Whenever you come together, each of you has a psalm, has a teaching, has a tongue, has a revelation, has an interpretation. Let all things be done for edification" (1 Cor 14:26 NKJV).

In Corinth the Church met in people's homes and, so, of necessity, numbers were limited in any gathering. This made it much easier for each person to participate than in contemporary gatherings of scores, hundreds, and even thousands. Paul reinforces this foundational concept of edification through diversity when he writes to the believers in Ephesus about being "knit together by what every joint supplies, according to the effective working by which every part does its share, causes growth of the body for the edifying of itself in love" (Eph 4:16 NKJV). God's chief purpose for the Church assembled is that it might become spiritually mature and that each of its members might contribute to that maturity while becoming spiritual adults. Each Christian contributes to the full development of the other members of the assembled congregation.

In all its gatherings, when edification is the underlying principle, the Church is spiritually strengthened week by week, minimizing confusion and disorder. Edification, therefore, becomes the standard by which contributions to the assembled saints are evaluated. When grandstanding and self-display replace edification as the motivating principle, confusion easily develops and minimal ministry takes place.

There also must be a governance structure of some kind. This may be very structured and hierarchical or loose and flat, with clear leadership but not much evidence of hierarchy. Policies are developed and levels of discipline are maintained through the governmental structure. This structure also provides the framework to conduct the business affairs of the congregation and ensure that the organizational side of the Church is healthy and adequately serving its needs. Governance structure can be seen as answering the question about where the authority of the Church resides and who has the right to exercise such authority.

Theologians have identified at least three forms of governance currently in use in the Church: episcopal, presbyterian, and congregational. In episcopal governance, generally considered the oldest form of governance, authority is vested in the leadership and is typical of Roman Catholics and Anglicans (Episcopalians in some countries). In presbyterian governance authority is vested in groups rather than individuals and there is only one class of clergy, as opposed to a clergy hierarchy. In congregational governance authority is vested in the assembled congregation, so democracy is an important principle. All congregations are encouraged to be self-governing, self-propagating, and self-supporting. The Bible has not mandated a specific form of governance, so the Church has freedom to adapt its form of governance to the culture in which it ministers.

There are also some fifty countries where Christians are actively persecuted. In some of these countries, Christians assemble in secret to avoid government sanction. In these situations, the assembled church can look radically different in form and function to the assembled church in countries where freedom of worship is unrestricted.

Since the Church, by its very nature, is a community of people, regular assembling together is essential for the Church to function effectively seven days a week. To summarize the reasons why we assemble, consider these points:

- To be equipped for ministry and built up or edified (Eph 4:12).
- To obey the instruction of Heb 10:25.
- To motivate and encourage one another (Heb 10:24–25).
- To warn each other so we are not deceived (Heb 3:13).
- To receive the ministry of others within the Church (1 Cor 12:21–27).

CHURCH DISTRIBUTED

When the Church is not assembled, then, obviously, it is distributed through the community. Whether assembled or distributed, the Church remains the Church.

There are 168 hours every week. Most Christians seem to spend less than four of those hours assembled with other Christians. Yet we seem to place the major emphasis on the time we spend assembled and extraordinarily little thought to the time when we are distributed throughout the community. When we are assembled there are numerous ways to serve: in the choir, teaching Sunday school, leading worship, as an usher, parking cars, leading a youth group, counselling, etc. How about when we are distributed through the community; do we still serve as the Church?

Much effort and theological reflection has gone into the time when the Church assembles. Much of the ecclesiological reflection available in print has focused exclusively on Church assembled. But how should the Church function when distributed? Should the four hours, or less, per week, when we come together, be our primary focus, or should that focus be directed to the time when we are penetrating every level of society? Is God's concern exclusively when we meet to worship, or does he have a vested interest in when we separate and go out into the world where we live and work?

When the focus is on the few hours that we are assembled, it is easy to develop a group of spectators who watch the professionals perform: the worship leader, singers, musicians, preachers. It is easy then to grow comfortable in the pew and become unconcerned the rest of the time. The Church is then limited to a few hours a week. This cannot be the Church that Jesus set out to build.

When we refocus to the time when we are distributed, no one can be a spectator, all must be participators because then church becomes a way of life rather than something we passively watch on Sunday mornings. Regretfully, the Church as institution does not seem to have sufficient sustainable connections with the outside world where the Church as organism spends most of its time.

So then, how can the Church be Church when distributed? There are three important biblical images that are pertinent in seeking to answer this question: salt, light, and holy nation.

Jesus declared in the Sermon on the Mount,

> You are the salt of the earth. But what good is salt if it has lost its flavor? Can you make it salty again? It will be thrown out and trampled underfoot as worthless. You are the light of the world, like a city on a hilltop that cannot be hidden. No one lights a lamp and then puts it under a basket. Instead, a lamp is placed on a stand, where it gives light to everyone in the house. In the same way, let your good deeds shine out for all to see, so that everyone will praise your heavenly Father.
> (Matt 5:13–16)

Notice a few simple things:

1. Jesus makes a statement of fact: "You are the salt of the earth," and "you are the light of the world." This is not something we aspire to. It is what we are, by nature, as Christians. We are

salt and we are light twenty-four hours a day, seven days a week, fifty-two weeks a year. There is no escaping this. Gathered or distributed, this is what we are. In the pulpit, in the civil service, in the market, in the school, in the village, in the city, in the home, this is who we are, present tense, now.

2. The "you" here is plural. Together, as the bride, we are salt and light. Gathered or distributed through society, collectively we remain salt and light. It is the cumulative result of our collective reality penetrating society seven days a week that brings salt and light into that society.

3. "Let your light shine" is an imperative command, not a suggestion. Jesus requires it of us. Our part is to obey.

4. How does that light shine? Through good deeds, service to others, and through lives committed to living out the reality of the inner change brought about by salvation so that men may see the glory of God. Wherever we serve, it is God's intention to penetrate the society at that point through our willingness to be his channels into the community where we live.

5. Salt and light, by their nature, are preservative, cleansing, and transformative. If we function as God intends us to function, then our society will begin to experience preservation and transformation as a natural result of the Church being the Church, distributed and serving society and gathering regularly to proclaim the gospel and worship. This divine methodology really works.

6. Salt and light are to impact everyone. The same God who makes the rain to fall on the just and the unjust expects that the salt and light of the Church will affect everyone in the society regardless of whether those persons are good or bad.

Add to this reality the gift of the Holy Spirit, given on the Day of Pentecost in Jerusalem, and the Church assembled or distributed is the most powerful organism on the face of the earth. It is a spiritual organism pulsating with the life of the Holy Spirit entering every office, business, government department, school, home, and aspect of society. This organism brings the power of the Triune God into every corner, breathing spiritual life into moribund social structures, challenging and dismantling evil structures while spreading the righteousness of Christ everywhere. Only the Church has this capacity. When we fail to grasp this, we miss the greatest opportunities we have to transform communities and change lives.

When Jesus died on the cross, Scripture tells us that "the veil of the temple was torn in two from top to bottom" (Matt 27:51). This signifies the access of every believer into the very presence of God the Father. It also relates to the Christian understanding that the Jewish temple in Jerusalem, destroyed by the Roman army in AD 70, has been replaced by the living temple of the *ecclesia*, the people who are the Church (Eph 2:19–22; 1 Cor 3:16–17; 6:19).

Ephesians 3:14–21 speaks of the believer having the Holy Spirit in the inner man, of Christ dwelling in the believer's heart and of the believer being "filled with all the fullness of God." Guthrie emphasizes that the totality of local believers is regarded as God's dwelling place,[1] which strongly implies that each Christian is part of the temple of God. As God dwelt in the holy of holies, so the Holy Spirit dwells in the *ecclesia*, the Church.

Indeed, in 1 Cor 6:16, Paul uses the Greek word *naos* which has been translated into English as temple. This word is narrow in meaning and has been applied almost exclusively to the holy of holies in the Jewish temple in Jerusalem. Consequently, when the Church, made up of "filled" believers, is distributed throughout the community, then the very presence of our awesome God, as expressed in the holy of holies, is brought into every place.

This is, in some ways, analogous to the Jews bringing the sacred ark of the covenant into the community. The ripped veil before the holy of holies, therefore, also signifies that God no longer resides over the mercy seat of the ark of the covenant, but has entered the community through his temple, the Church, the community of believers.

---

1. Guthrie, *New Testament Theology*, 748.

As stated above, the Church distributed brings the salt and light that Jesus speaks of in Matt 5:13–16 into direct contact with the society. It is also when distributed that the service of the royal priesthood (1 Pet 2:9) can be effectively delivered throughout society.

The Hebrew concept of *kavanah* is pertinent. *Kavanah* is the mindset for prayer and carries the sense of being profoundly conscious of God in all we do: at prayer, in studying the Scriptures, in performing acts of compassion, and in pursuing our various professions and vocations. Ideally, each is to be done with a profound awareness of the presence of God, who desires to speak and work through us at every moment. It is this consciousness of the presence of God in our lives, taken into every facet of society, that will transform families, communities, and nations.

When Jesus was incarnated, he stepped off his throne of glory, entered human flesh, and was born into our world as the consummate expression of God's love for mankind. Similarly, there is a sense in which the disciple of Jesus incarnates his master's teachings into his lifestyle so that there is a visible expression of God's love and righteousness in the community where that disciple lives. Any profession of Christianity that does not encompass, through the disciples of Jesus, a growing measure of incarnation of the principles, precepts, and promises of God, in the Bible, eventually appears hypocritical. The power of a Christian incarnating the truths of God, lived out in everyday life, is immeasurable.

Both Matthew and Luke record Jesus' metaphor of the kingdom of heaven being like yeast, which is hidden in bread and affects the entire batch of dough (Matt 13:33; Luke 13:20–21). Part of the enigma that is Church is that the Church foreshadows the kingdom, but embodies the kingdom in our generation. If then the Church, God's people, carries the power of spiritual yeast into society, it can only be effective where the yeast penetrates the dough. The yeast must be in the dough to affect the dough.

Carter chronicles the yeasting of society by the Church of the Nazarene in Barbados, stating, "The counterbalancing work of the church, calling men and women to live productive, wholesome lives is of paramount importance for the development of any community, and the country has made enormous strides in its human resource development because of the work and interests of the churches."[2]

God, speaking through the Old Testament prophet Jeremiah, as the Hebrews went into captivity in Babylon, encourages them to "work for the peace and prosperity of the city where I sent you into exile" (Jer 29:7). This is a powerful principle for the Church distributed throughout all levels in society.

An honest reading of Scripture concludes that the gospel is meant to be transformational, transforming the individual, the family, the community, and, ultimately, the nation. Being salt and light is not a spiritual position of great reverence and ceremonial importance. Being salt and light is the down-to-earth, practical outworking in daily life of the teaching and principles of Jesus in such a way that change results in our own lives and in the lives of the people with whom we interact in the society in which we are immersed.

Once we define Church as a community of people, we need to enable and empower these people to function as Church (salt and light) in society. We have restricted Church to Sunday morning at a specific time, in a specific location, with a specific program or order of service. Church remains Church every morning, but we have been conditioned, by our mindset, to equip the Church to function when it is gathered on Sunday morning, and have not equipped it to function as Church, all the time, distributed through society.

We are rediscovering the truth that anything done in the name of Christ, in the name of God's love, is ministry. Consequently, we must broaden and enrich the concept of personal ministry. We must bless, affirm, and be willing to release people into areas that may not directly benefit the local congregation, but expand the influence and ministry of the Church throughout society. Every profession is a way to serve God, a means of ministry to enable

---

2. Carter, *Moulding Communities*, 181.

those who do not know God to experience him in the living embodiment of a Christian living out practical faith daily.

When assembled to worship, that is the Church gathered. When Christians leave the building to go about our normal business, that is the Church distributed. Gathered or distributed the Church is still the Church and always remains the visible expression of God in the community.

One of the clear lessons from the COVID-19 pandemic is that when the Church assembled is closed and prohibited from gathering, the Church distributed can never be closed, but continues ministry at every level of society. May we learn that lesson and seek God for the creativity we need to be the Church distributed every day, in the places where God has planted us throughout the economic, political, and social sectors of society.

Scripture seems clear that the Church Jesus declared he would build was not intended to be an end dressed in ornate buildings and repetitive ritual becoming merely another social organization where people of the same mind gather.

The late Sir Winston Churchill, at the time prime minister of Great Britain, addressed the Canadian House of Commons in December 1941, during World War II. A quote from his well-known speech could be applied to the twenty-first century Church. "There is no room now for the dilettante, the weakling, for the shirker or the sluggard. The mine, the factory, the dockyard, the salt sea waves, the fields to till, the home, the hospital, the chair of the scientist, the pulpit of the preacher, from the highest to the humblest tasks, are all at equal honor, all have their part to play."[3]

---

3. Humes, *Wit and Wisdom*, 128.

CHAPTER 5

Changing the Way We Think

"Don't copy the behavior and customs of this world, but let God transform you into a new person by changing the way you think" (Rom 12:2).

Few people seem to be aware that how we think is conditioned by thought patterns and assumptions that we have imbibed throughout our lives. This is called a worldview. It is the mental patterns we have developed and through which we filter everything we see and hear to attach meaning to all that is around us. The word "worldview" is said to have developed in English from a German word which means "life perspective" or "way of seeing."

These thought patterns first begin to be shaped by the family in which we have been born. Parents, siblings, grandparents, aunts, uncles, and cousins are the early sources of what we grow to think is right or wrong. A simple example can be found in those who say that their parents were members of a specific political party or church and, so, they, themselves, will remain in that party or church for the rest of their lives. This demonstrates how strong thought patterns are established from early in our lives.

School is also an important source from which we develop thought patterns. These patterns are steadily reinforced through education from kindergarten to university. Education shapes and reshapes our worldview. Education can reinforce or destroy the thought patterns that we developed through family influence and replace them with new ones.

During those formative years of childhood and teenage realities, friends also begin to impact our thought patterns for good or bad. The importance attached to these friends determines how much they will influence our thought patterns and whether that influence is negative or positive.

The national culture in which we grow up is another strong shaper of thought patterns. National culture is inherently important in how we define ourselves and how we look out at the world around us. As one travels the world, the difference in culture and how that impacts worldview is glaringly obvious, even if we do not look for it.

Growing older, the experiences we live through also shape our inner thought patterns. These experiences positively or negatively impact us in the mind. Often, without even being conscious, lifelong changes are imbedded within us and, then, become how we determine truth and error, likes and dislikes.

History also has a significant impact on how thought processes are shaped. For example, the issues of African chattel slavery and European colonialism have overwhelmingly impacted thought patterns, often in destructive ways, in former European colonies. Those historical societal structures have shaped much of the way thought patterns have been developed in the colonized, as well as the colonizers. Since it is the victors who write history, the thought patterns established by that history often must be broken down to build new thought patterns that include the realities of the vanquished and provide a positive path forward.

When persons become disciples of Jesus, then the Scriptures become a significant tool in reshaping thought patterns. The principles and precepts of the Bible are often at odds with the thought patterns learned up to the point of conversion and, sometimes, this engenders very real internal struggles. Changing established thought patterns (worldview) can be emotionally and psychologically painful, even though necessary.

Each local congregation has its own unique culture, the way things are done, the words that are used, the attitudes that are projected, and so much more make up that culture. Sadly, some of these cultures are more destructive than constructive and pastoral abuse is a clear, unfortunate reality today. Those church cultures have a further impact on refining our thought patterns.

Those thought patterns are sometimes described as beliefs. It has been suggested that as we pass everything we think through those beliefs, we, in fact, see more through our beliefs than through our eyes. This makes our thought patterns critical to our success or failure.

There are several positive factors about worldview, our thought patterns. They form the basis by which we determine what is objective truth. They provide the internal standards by which we subconsciously measure everything. In this way, these thought patterns determine for us what is our reality. They also provide the basis from which we decide how and when we will act on anything. A positive worldview can also give us hope and direction as we chart our course through life.

There can be some extremely negative aspects of worldview. It can cause us to misunderstand issues with which we are confronted. If our inner thought patterns are, for some reason, askew, then our understanding of reality is skewed without us being conscious that this is so.

Our thought patterns can also disrupt our ability to understand the Bible, as our thoughts have become conditioned by our worldview to see certain things and not see others. Reading the Bible over a period of years, many people still find fresh insights and sometimes wonder why they never saw certain things before. Part of the reason is how the thought patterns have been conditioned, over time, to process information through the mind. This can mean that we do not grasp important issues and precepts which are fundamental to Christian development. These thought patterns can also squeeze our thinking into predetermined molds, where our faith is limited and our spiritual growth stunted.

From this background Paul enjoins us to "let God transform you into a new person by changing the way you think" (Rom 12:2). It can be incredibly difficult to change thought patterns. Usually, divine assistance is necessary.

The Greek word used here for "transform" is the same word from which we get the English word "metamorphosis." That word is used to describe the process by which a caterpillar changes into a butterfly, going from an earthbound worm crawling on its belly to a thing of beauty rising to the tops of the trees and flowers. Such a metamorphosis needs to take place in our thought patterns. As thought patterns change, transformation takes place and actions are revolutionized so that difference is obvious in all manner of ways.

The key question, then, is how can thought patterns, our worldview, be changed? It does not happen by just going to the front of the church building, towards the end of a worship service, and having some pastor or leader lay on hands and pray. It is much more a process of spiritual development and renewal.

In Rom 12:1, Paul links a total commitment to God, becoming a living sacrifice, to the process of inner thought pattern metamorphosis. Such a complete surrender goes against the individualism embedded in the Western thought patterns learned growing up in homes, schools, and communities. Yet, it is the pathway to truly radical changes in how we think. There will be times of struggle, times when it seems impossible to move forward. Unless this metamorphosis is embraced as an inward, ongoing work of the Holy Spirit, we are doomed to mediocre spiritual development with little or no impact in the community around us.

As already stated, the Church, the people, are called to be salt and light, impacting the societies in which we live. To get there we need a radical change in worldview, our thought patterns. "Let the Spirit renew your thoughts and attitudes" (Eph 4:23). The writer of the book of Proverbs warns, "For as he thinks within himself, so is he" (Prov 23:7 TLV). It is critical that this area of life goes through the metamorphosis Paul speaks about in Rom 12:1–2.

How thoughts impact lives is demonstrated in this old saying many were taught as children, "Sow a thought, reap an action. Sow an action, reap a habit. Sow a habit, reap a character. Sow a character, reap a destiny." There's another old saying that makes the point as well. "Take the 'h' from habit and 'abit' is still there. Take away the 'a' and 'bit' is still there. Take away the 'b' and 'it' is still there." Such is the power of the worldview that has established our personal way of thinking.

The presence and power of the Holy Spirit can, and should, enable radical change in the way we think.

CHAPTER 6

Character Reconstruction

CHRISTIANITY, WHEN PERSONALLY EMBRACED through a dynamic faith, has a powerful effect on the inside of the individual. As Christians are distributed through the community, it is their living testimony of transformation and personal integrity that is a primary enabler of the salt and light within them to impact their societal environment.

Nothing has a greater negative impact than a Christian whose character is not continually being transformed by the power of God.

Paul outlines character traits that are inextricably linked to the operation of the Holy Spirit in the lives of believers. "But the Holy Spirit produces this kind of fruit in our lives: love, joy, peace, patience, kindness, goodness, faithfulness, gentleness, and self-control" (Gal 5:22–23).

The fact that these nine characteristics are described as fruit indicates an especially important characteristic of how they are manifested. Fruits automatically grow on fruit trees once the trees have access to water and nutrients in the soil where they are planted. If the soil is arid and infertile, the tree will not be able to grow or produce fruit.

The verses in Gal 5 are clear that "the Holy Spirit produces this kind of fruit in our lives." It is our connection, indeed infilling, with the Holy Spirit that gives us access to the spiritual water and nutrients that cause these fruits to grow in our lives. They are natural outcomes of a close walk with God. Like the fruit trees, we do not struggle and strain to produce these characteristics in our lives. They grow in direct correlation to our relationship with God, the Holy Spirit. A soul thirsty for God drinks of the water of the Holy Spirit, and the fruit begins to grow. The fruit develops as a direct result of the individual being indwelled by the Holy Spirit.

Love is the first fruit listed. Many have postulated that the other eight fruits in the list are merely expressions of love. That may be the case, but a reflection on each fruit is profitable.

The Greek word here translated "love" is not known widely outside of the Christian Scriptures. It is described as the highest form of love and is defined extensively in 1 Cor 13. Even a cursory perusal of that passage makes it crystal clear that we are not capable, in ourselves, of producing such an all-embracing, selfless love. It is produced within us by the Holy Spirit as we surrender our lives to him on an ongoing basis.

The apostle John summed it up succinctly when he wrote, "As we live in God, our love grows more perfect" (1 John 4:17). Such love is the bedrock of who we are as the Church in the twenty-first century. Paul asserts, "Three things will last forever—faith, hope, and love—and the greatest of these is love" (1 Cor 13:13). In the record of the New Testament Gospels, Jesus extended real love through his life and ministry to people in need around him. He reserved rebuke and reprimand for the religious leaders of his day. Jesus stated that love for each other within the Church would be the identifying mark of the Christian (John 13:35).

Joy is the second fruit in the Gal 5 list. This is a deep inner reality that is not dependent on outward circumstances. It is an active delight. It draws from the indwelling Holy Spirit "for the joy of the Lord is your strength" (Neh 8:10). Proverbs 17:22 declares, "A cheerful heart is good medicine." The prophet Isaiah asserts, "I am overwhelmed with joy in the Lord my God" (Isa 61:10). The apostle Paul exhorts us, "Always be full of joy in the Lord. I say it again, rejoice" (Phil 4:4).

Such joy is not manufactured or a pretence. It is the fruit of a human spirit enraptured with the Holy Spirit, living in his presence and expressing the living water from deep within.

Peace is the natural outflow of the first two fruits. The Greek word for "peace" used here is similar to the Hebrew *shalom*. It conveys not only the absence of anxiety but the sense of wholeness, of being at rest, the fullness of wellbeing, having a harmony within that rests in the inner presence of the Holy Spirit and not on outward circumstances. Paul sums it up this way, "Then you will experience God's peace, which exceeds anything we can understand. His peace will guard your hearts and minds as you live in Christ Jesus" (Phil 4:7).

Such peace flowing from the relationship with the Holy Spirit banishes the anxieties that rear their heads in the dark stillness of the night. Such peace may be shaken by the attacks of our spiritual enemies, but it cannot be diminished or broken once we are drawing our resources from the indwelling Holy Spirit. Such peace is a natural outflow from the Holy Spirit.

John quotes Jesus in his gospel as saying, "I am leaving you with a gift, peace of mind and heart. And the peace I give is a gift the world cannot give. So don't be troubled or afraid" (John 14:27). The prophet Isaiah, speaking to God, declares, "You will keep in perfect peace all who trust in you, all whose thoughts are fixed on you" (Isa 26:3). Paul, writing to the Christians in Thessalonica, prays, "Now may the Lord of peace himself give you his peace at all times and in every situation" (2 Thess 3:16).

This peace has already been packaged and paid for. It was purchased through Jesus' death on the cross and is made available to us through the "packaging" of the Holy Spirit. It is a natural outcome of building a life-long relationship with the third person of the Trinity.

This leads into *patience*, rendered long-suffering in some English translations of the Scriptures. The Greek carries the sense of patient endurance, an uncommon character trait in the twenty-first century—where the instant process of technology makes waiting seem onerous. Yet patience is a quality of character that is useful and essential.

Paul wrote to the congregations in Corinth during a time when Christians were widely persecuted, "In everything we do, we show that we are true ministers of God. We patiently endure troubles and hardships and calamities of every kind" (2 Cor 6:4–5). In Col 1:11, Paul links the character traits of endurance, patience, and joy. He also writes to the Ephesians, "Be patient with each other, making allowance for each other's faults because of your love" (Eph 4:2). The concept of patient endurance is also the main point of Gal 6:9 even though those specific words are not used, "So let's not get tired of doing what is good. At just the right time we will reap a harvest of blessing if we don't give up." Proverbs 25:15 states, "Patience can persuade a prince," while Eccl 7:8 affirms, "Patience is better than pride."

Kindness, translated as gentleness in some English versions, is the next to make the list. The Greek word used here carries the sense of benevolence, a usefulness to others. It can be described as generosity of spirit. Paul exhorts the Christians at Ephesus to "be kind to each other" (Eph 4:32). To the Colossians he urges, "You must clothe yourselves with tender hearted mercy, kindness, humility, gentleness, and patience" (Col 3:12).

Paul reminds us that God "has showered his kindness on us" (Eph 1:8), thereby establishing the characteristic that we can and should grow into as we grow in the image of our heavenly Father. The prophet Zechariah, in the Hebrew Scriptures (which Christians call the Old Testament), exhorts us to "show mercy and kindness to one another" (Zech 7:9). Acts of kindness bring their own recompense, "Your kindness will reward you" (Prov 11:17), and are refreshing to the hearts of recipients (Phlm 1:7).

As kindness grows, so will *goodness*. The Greek word translated here as "goodness" carries the sense of generosity flowing from a right relationship with God rather than just moral goodness. The stress is more on the generosity of God than the morality of a human.

Paul writes to the Christians in Rome about being "full of goodness" (Rom 15:14), and Peter writes, "you can show others the goodness of God" (1 Pet 2:9) Perhaps the best-known verse on goodness is Ps 23:6, "Surely your goodness and unfailing love will pursue me all the days of my life."

Faithfulness is the seventh character trait in the list. It is, essentially, trustworthiness and reliability towards our God and our fellowman. This, too, is a basic trait of the God we serve. A deepening relationship with God, the Holy Spirit, will lead to the developing reality of faithfulness in the character of the Christian. Jesus taught, "If you are faithful in little things, you will be faithful in large ones" (Luke 16:10), suggesting that, as his disciples, Jesus will give us smaller opportunities to grow in faithfulness before moving us on to greater areas of trustworthiness.

Paul taught that we must "be entirely trustworthy and good," for it is then that we "will make the teaching about God our Savior attractive in every way" (Titus 2:10). As Paul neared the date of his execution under the orders of Roman Emperor Nero, he was able to say, among other things, "I have remained faithful" (2 Tim 4:7).

Gentleness is the penultimate trait in this list, translated as meekness in some English Bible versions. Perhaps the concept of humility captures the intent of this word in the Greek. Humility is not weakness but has been characterized as strength under control. It is a quality highly prized by God, who said to the prophet Isaiah, "I will bless those who have humble and contrite hearts" (Isa 66:2).

Paul challenges Christians to "always be humble and gentle" (Eph 4:2). He also writes to the Colossians, "Since God chose you to be the holy people he loves, you must clothe yourselves with tender hearted mercy, kindness, humility, gentleness, and patience" (Col 3:12). Jesus, in the great Sermon on the Mount, said, "God blesses those who are humble, for they will inherit the whole earth" (Matt 5:5). The prophet Micah also declares emphatically, "The Lord has told you what is good, and this is what he requires of you: to do what is right, to love mercy, and to walk humbly with your God" (Mic 6:8).

The final personal quality in this list is *self-control*, or temperance in some of the older English versions. Self-control is a critical character trait for any Christian, as it is the key quality in controlling the passions and lusts of the flesh. It is the grace by which we dominate the allure of sin. Lack of self-control is exhibited in eating, gambling, drug addictions (including alcohol abuse), pursuing illicit sexual liaisons, and so much more.

Lack of self-control can be devastating. "An evil man is held captive by his own sins; they are ropes that catch and hold him. He will die for lack of self-control; he will be lost because of his great foolishness" (Prov 5:22–23). Proverbs 25:28 puts it starkly, "A person without self-control is like a city with broken-down walls." The apostle Peter, in the first of his epistles, says that one of the things that should supplement our faith is self-control (1 Pet 1:5–7).

This list can be daunting in considering the character development each Christian faces, as none are perfect and all will see areas where there needs to be improvement. No one is asked to do this in their own strength and effort. That will only lead to discouragement and an overwhelming sense of guilt when we fall short.

Remember, it is in developing our personal relationship with God the Holy Spirit that these character traits are developed within our lives. It is not expected that we will struggle on our own to live this way. It is a developmental process. Do not despair or move into guilt when it seems that aspects of these character traits are miniscule or even absent. It is a process.

Do not be discouraged when you go through difficult circumstances. It is in those circumstances that God is shaping character and developing these fruits on the inside. It's not a flash of blinding light or an instantaneous transformation. Throughout life God shapes and fashions according to his purpose, and builds within the character that which honors and glorifies him.

This does not mean that the Christian has no responsibility. The responsibility of the disciples of Jesus is to deliberately cultivate our relationship with the Father, Son, and Holy Spirit through prayer, the study of our sacred Scriptures, and assembling regularly with other Christian believers, that we may build up each other

(Heb 10:25). It is also the Christian's responsibility to take personal action, as guided by the Bible, and deliberately work through changes that are needed as we progress through life's journey.

This is not a sprint, but a lifelong marathon of spiritual growth in grace and knowledge of God. Christians are at different points of our spiritual journey, so let us help each other further along the way.

CHAPTER 7

Called to Be Servants

GRASPING THE REALITY THAT we, the people, are the Church and that we are undergoing character reconstruction, and in the process of changing the way we think, all comes together in being the Church distributed throughout the community to serve that community in which we live. We are called to be servants.

Jesus was clear about this. There really can be no misunderstanding his words. As his disciples discussed among themselves which of them would be the greatest in Jesus' kingdom, he repeatedly pointed them to servanthood. In Mark 10:43–45, Jesus is recorded as saying, "Whoever wants to be a leader among you must be your servant, and whoever wants to be first among you must be the slave of everyone else. For even the Son of Man came not to be served but to serve others." Jesus sharply contrasts the way the world around him operated and how his disciples were to operate. There is no mystery here.

In Matt 20:26–28, it is again recorded that Jesus said, "But among you it will be different. Whoever wants to be a leader among you must be your servant, and whoever wants to be first among you must become your slave. For even the Son of Man came not to be served but to serve others." If Jesus came to serve, then, as his disciples, the Church must also serve, whether assembled in buildings for corporate acts of worship or distributed through the community in daily life.

Luke also records that Jesus said,

> In this world the kings and great men lord it over their people, yet they are called 'friends of the people.' But among you it will be different. Those who are the greatest among you should take the lowest rank, and the leader should be like a servant. Who is more important, the one who sits at the table or the one who serves? The one who sits at the table, of course. But not here! For I am among you as one who serves. (Luke 22:25–27)

Note the three emphatic words, "But not here!"

This instruction came during the Last Supper, the very night Jesus was betrayed, arrested, and, subsequently, sentenced to death. It is also part of that incredible evening when Jesus stooped to wash his disciples' feet and then commanded them to do as he had done. Interestingly, the biblical time line suggests that even Judas had his feet washed by Jesus. It is, therefore, mandatory that the Church translate this principle of servanthood into the reality of our homes, workplaces, and social interactions. It cannot just be an annual ritual during Holy Week, but must be a principle inculcated in our daily lives. When the Holy Spirit ensured that something as radical as this was recorded at least three times, it is fitting that we pay serious attention.

Even the apostle Peter encouraged Christians, "All of you, serve each other in humility" (1 Pet 5:5), while the apostle Paul frequently refers to serving and being servants in his epistles.

Some three decades or more ago, Robert Greenleaf coined the term "servant leader" in his writings for management and leadership in society outside of the institutional church. Yet this was a concept taught and modelled by Jesus almost two thousand years ago. It is a principle of his kingdom. In this kingdom true greatness is found in serving, not being served. It is the total opposite of the world system in which we live.

If the spiritual kingdom into which Christians have been transplanted is characterized by servanthood, then we are called to serve wherever we are placed in society, whatever our role or position in the spiritual, corporate, public, or political worlds in which we earn our salaries and apply our God-given gifts, talents, and abilities. As the Church distributed, through the society, we bring the principles and character of Jesus and his teachings wherever we are through the way we live, in everything we do. We are called to be radically different as this principle of servanthood cuts across much of the way the world system operates.

In the prayer which seems to have closed out the Last Supper and is recorded in John 17:1–25, there are a couple of sentences very pertinent to this discussion.

In John 17:15, Jesus prays to God the Father concerning his disciples, "I'm not asking you to take them out of the world, but to keep them safe from the evil one." Then, in verse 18, he prays, "I am sending them into the world." So, we are not called to live removed from the world, but to be in the world, even as the Holy Spirit makes us separate by transforming our character, empowering us to serve in the supernatural, and changing the mindset we developed prior to coming to Christ. Clearly, we "do not belong to the world" (verse 14), but it is in the world that we are called to serve.

Looking at the whole of verse 18, Jesus makes an important point, "Just as you sent me into the world, I am sending them into the world." This, then, raises the question, how was Jesus sent into the world? Philippians 2:5–8 gives some challenging insight into how Jesus came into the world. This passage has been much discussed and disputed through the centuries of theological development. Acknowledging that, here are a few simple points.

Jesus "gave up his divine privileges" (Phil 2:7). The KJV translates this phrase, "made himself of no reputation." The TLV translation reads, "He emptied Himself." When Jesus entered earth in human form, he did so as the son of a carpenter and grew up in a small village, which archaeologists say was probably comprised of little more than fifty homes. There was none of the majesty and glory of heaven evident in his circumstances. The magi (or wise men) went to the palace of Herod the Great expecting that Jesus, a king, would have been born there. The record we have of that visit does not indicate if they were surprised to be redirected to a simple home in Bethlehem.

It is interesting to note here that Jesus selects, for his purposes, people and things considered to be nothing and uses them to confound those considered important (1 Cor 1:27–28).

Not only did Jesus give up everything as God the Son to take human form, he also "took the humble position of a slave" (Phil 2:7). We've seen above that he pointed this out very clearly to his disciples as they argued about who should have the best places in his kingdom and commanded them to take the place of a servant rather than lord.

Then Jesus "humbled himself in obedience to God" (Phil 2:8). Obedience can be very humbling. As children, we sometimes struggled with obedience to our parents. Those who are dog lovers have watched, sometimes, as their adored canine has struggled to submit to the commands of its master and owner. The Gospels record for us how Jesus struggled in prayer in Gethsemane, leading up to his arrest. He knew the suffering he would face in the coming hours and asked, if possible, to be released from what he knew was coming. Yet he concluded his time of prayer with full submission and obedience to his Father's will (John 22:42). He was totally submitted to the will of God the Father.

Then Phil 2:8 says he died. Jesus taught his disciples, "If you refuse to take up your cross and follow me, you are not worthy of being mine. If you cling to your life, you will lose it; but if you give up your life for me, you will find it" (Matt 10:38–39).

Philippians 2:5 says, "You must have the same attitude that Christ Jesus had." The KJV translates the word "attitude" as "mind," and the NIV as "mindset." Christians are commanded to think the same way Jesus thought. Therefore, the Holy Spirit works on transforming our worldview, our mindset (Rom 12:1–2). It is no easy task, but an adventure in spiritual growth for every Christian.

This is all linked into being salt and light in a world that seems anxious to push God aside and live with moral abandon. It is in having the attitude of Jesus, and understanding all that being his servant in our world today requires, that we can shed the light of the gospel for all to encounter. Anything less misses the mark Jesus set for us.

As several theologians from different cultures and countries have pointed out, there is a sense in which we incarnate the truths of the gospel in the way we live. As Jesus incarnated the divine in the human, so we incarnate, draw in practical ways into our daily lives, the reality of the transformational power of the gospel in the way we live and interact with those around us.

Distributed throughout society, Christians are agents of a spiritual kingdom and incarnate the truths of Scripture in their lifestyles and in interaction with others who are Christians as well as persons who are far from God.

This servanthood is not to be confused with being servile. We are not called to be obsequious, cringing, fawning, or abject. The servanthood of a Christian is a service to others empowered by the Holy Spirit, with a changing mindset that seeks primarily to obey God and express his love in serving. In the same way that we understand the meekness that Jesus taught is power under control, so the servanthood he taught as a principle of life is the power of the Holy Spirit expressed in humility and love.

Rev. Martin Luther King Jr. epitomized servanthood in his activism against racial injustice in the United States of America. He practiced nonviolence and urged his colleagues to do the same. His was a life of service and he paid the ultimate price, but his servanthood laid the foundation for national change.

Nelson Mandela, early in life, took up the fight against apartheid in South Africa and was sent to jail for nearly three decades. On his release from jail, he chose the path of service and reconciliation, leading the way for the nation to begin emerging from injustice and rampant, violent racism.

William Wilberforce committed forty years of his life fighting in the British House of Commons for the abolition of the slave trade and, subsequently, the emancipation of slaves in the British Empire. Success came at the end of his life. Wilberforce, at the same time, championed more than sixty other causes, including reforms in factory labor, immigration statutes, equitable weights and measures, child-labor laws, farm labor, and colonial administration. His was a life of servanthood that helped transform Britain and its empire.

In the twenty-first century, Christian servanthood remains the essence of demonstrating the gospel of Jesus in a world that seems anxious to forget him.

CHAPTER 8

A Royal Priesthood

ONE OF THE CRITICAL beliefs emphasized during the Protestant Reformation was the priesthood of all believers: the reality that each believer has access to God through the High Priesthood of Jesus Christ himself.

The late Rev. Kermit Hanson, pastor of Berean Bible Church, at that time, on Passage Road in Bridgetown, Barbados, strongly emphasized in converts' class that evangelical Christians did not call their leaders priests because of the firm belief that every Christian is a royal priest. This belief rests on 1 Pet 2:5, 9, where the apostle Peter applies to the Church, that universal company of believers, the designation first given, by God, to the people of Israel in Exod 19:5–6 and Isa 61:6.

ROYAL PRIESTS AND THE MELCHIZEDEKIAN ORDER

Monarchs who exercised priestly roles were not uncommon in the ancient world. Many kings also served as the high priest of their religion. There are no real contemporaries in the Western world. Perhaps the closest today is the pope, who, as head of the Roman Catholic Church, is also the ruler of the miniscule country called the Vatican State.

Additionally, the monarch of the United Kingdom is the titular head of the Church of England and bears the title Defender of the Faith. Ironically, that title was conferred on King Henry VIII by Pope Leo X in 1521, when King Henry wrote a vigorous defense of Roman Catholic doctrine in response to Martin Luther's challenges of Catholic dogma. It was rescinded by Pope Paul III when England broke with the Church of Rome a few years later. The English Parliament, subsequently, restored the title to the monarch in 1544 and it has been borne by the monarchs of England, and subsequently, the United Kingdom, ever since. Even King Charles III, during his coronation in 2023, acknowledged that he carried that title and sacred responsibility.

Melchizedek, king of Salem, appears in Gen 14:18–20 and is clearly identified there as a king and a priest. Hebrews 7:2 (TLV) translates the name as meaning "King of Righteousness" and the title "King of Salem" as "King of Shalom," or peace. Some linguists have also pointed out the name can mean "my king is righteous." This is the first biblical reference to a priest and king. It is therefore important. Hebrews 7:1–24 makes it clear that Melchizedek's order of priesthood is greater than the Aaronic and Levitical priesthood, and continues forever.

There is ongoing discussion on who Melchizedek could have been. At the least, he was a priest of the Most High God of the Old Testament and was recognized as such by Abraham. He is certainly a type of the Messiah, the quintessential royal priest who would save his people from their sins. Morris, after discussing various theories on the identity of Melchizedek, represents one school of thinking among evangelical Christians when he states that it does seem that the interpretation most consistent with biblical literalism is the recognition of Melchizedek as a manifestation to Abram of the preincarnate Jesus, the eternal priestly mediator between man and God. If that is so, the royal priestly order of Melchizedek becomes much more significant.[1]

King David associates himself with the Melchizedekian order of royal priesthood in Ps 110. Accepted by most commentators

---

1. Morris, *Genesis*, 321.

as a messianic psalm with ultimate application to Jesus, it had an immediate application to David as the Melchizedekian royal priest ruling Israel from the city of Melchizedek: Salem, or Jerusalem. Hebrews 7 applies the psalm directly to Jesus. Some commentators see David in his priestly role when the ark of the covenant is brought from the home of Obed-Edom to Jerusalem (1 Chr 15–16). Merrill says of King David that, on that day, he led the festive procession dressed as a priest and clearly functioned in that capacity.[2] David's priesthood was not like the Aaronic priesthood, but he did have a priest's role in leading his people in the ways of YHWH.

David provides the human linkage from Adam through Abraham to Christ, making Jesus the King of Israel, who will sit forever on the throne of David. David also provides the linkage between Melchizedek and Christ, an everlasting order of priesthood higher than that of Aaron and the Levites. The Melchizedekian order of priesthood is the only biblical order of priesthood into which the gentiles could be initiated. Receiving Jesus Christ as one's Savior and accepting his sacrifice on the cross for the personal forgiveness of one's sins provides the believer with access into the royal priesthood, a priesthood after the order of Melchizedek, of which Jesus is the high priest. Christians are then the priests who reign with Christ, exercising spiritual rulership and authority in this life and eternity.

PRIVILEGE OF BEING A PRIEST

Among the greatest privileges of being a priest is the access that this grants into the very presence of God. One of the miraculous events that accompanied the death of Jesus on the cross was the tearing of the temple veil from the top to the bottom (Matt 27:51). This veil separated the holy place from the holy of holies (Exod 26:31–35) in the tabernacle of Moses. In the temple, at the time of

---

2. Merrill, *Kingdom of Priests*, 246.

Jesus, there was a wall with two doors and the veil covered part of the wall and the doors.

The holy place contained the table of showbread, the altar of incense, and the lamp stand. The holy of holies contained the ark of the covenant and a visible expression of the glory of God until God dramatically departed the temple, as recorded by Ezekiel (Ezek 10:1–19). Only the Aaronic high priest could pass through the veil into the holy of holies, the very presence of God, and, then, only once a year on Yom Kippur, the Day of Atonement.

The veil of the temple has been described as an elaborately woven fabric of seventy-two twisted plaits of twenty-four threads each, being sixty feet long and thirty feet wide.[3] Only God could have torn such a piece of fabric from top to bottom. This clearly symbolizes that every believer from that moment on has been granted access directly to God the Father.

Heb 10:19–22 elucidates,

> Therefore, brethren, having boldness to enter the Holiest by the blood of Jesus, by a new and living way which he consecrated for us, through the veil, that is, his flesh, and having a High Priest over the house of God, let us draw near with a true heart in full assurance of faith, having our hearts sprinkled from an evil conscience and our bodies washed with pure water (NKJV).

What an incredible privilege that we, so often, now take for granted.

The tearing of the veil in the temple also signified that God would no longer dwell in a building made by human hands. Instead, the apostle Paul states, "For we are the temple of the living God. As God said: 'I will live in them and walk among them. I will be their God, and they will be my people'" (2 Cor 6:16). As royal priests, Christians not only have access to the very presence of God but that presence dwells within them.

Paul expands further when he states that Christians are "empowered with inner strength through his Spirit" (Eph 3:16), that

---

3. Wilkins, *Matthew*, 904.

"Christ will make his home in your hearts as you trust in him" (Eph 4:17), and that Christians "may be made complete with all the fullness of life and power that comes from God" (Eph 3:18). (This will be discussed further in the final chapter.) Such a personal and corporate reality is a privilege beyond compare with anything else known to man! If God dwells in us, then we take his presence everywhere we go. As Christians live, labor, and minister in every facet of society, the presence of God is spread throughout the length and breadth of that society.

From the situation where only one man could enter God's presence, and only once a year, to a reality that every believer has access into that same presence of God, and that God himself dwells within the believer, is incredible. It is indeed an awesome privilege.

RESPONSIBILITY IN BEING A PRIEST

As always, with privileges come responsibilities. Having access directly into the presence of God carries the responsibility of a mediatorial role. While there is but "one Mediator who can reconcile God and humanity—the man Christ Jesus" (1 Tim 2:5) in terms of Savior and Redeemer, Christians intercede with God on behalf of their fellowmen and speak to their fellowmen on behalf of God. That intermediary role is critical in carrying out the commission given to the apostles by Jesus to make disciples, and through the apostles to the Church in all generations. Making disciples has an element of the mediatorial role as we share God's gospel and invite all people everywhere to respond to the sacrifice of Christ upon the cross.

The very nature of a biblical priest's ministry is the offering of sacrifices. A sacrifice, in this context, is something offered to God by a priest. Christians, as royal priests, are called upon to offer spiritual sacrifices (1 Pet 2:5).

Paul urges all Christians to "let [your bodies] be a living sacrifice ... [which] is truly the way to worship him" (Rom 12:1). It is the Christian's reasonable service because "God bought you with a high price. So you must honor God with your body" (1 Cor 6:20).

Just about every religion in New Testament times offered animal sacrifices. Paul's imagery in challenging his readers to become a living sacrifice would have been instantly understood by his readers. Though redeemed by Christ's shed blood, believers still live in an imperfect body. The only reasonable thing to do is to surrender that body to Christ and to allow him to have lordship in every aspect of our being. Having already discussed the reality of God's presence within the believer, it is crucial that we make our bodies a living sacrifice that his presence may shine through us and impact our families, neighbors, workmates, and all with whom we come into contact.

Normally the priest would offer something else as a sacrifice. In Rom 12:1, the royal priest offers himself as the sacrifice. Typically, a sacrifice would die and then be laid upon an altar to be consumed by fire. Here, death is central as the Christian dies to self and sin, but life is the overriding principle as the Christian then lives "by trusting in the Son of God, who loved me and gave himself for me" (Gal 2:20). A glorious paradox lived out daily in the lives of millions of believers, and part of the wonderful enigma that is Church.

Another sacrifice offered by the royal priests is a "continual sacrifice of praise to God, proclaiming our allegiance to his name" (Heb 13:15). The praise and thanksgiving offering was a major sacrifice of flour, oil, and leavened and unleavened bread (Lev 7:11–21), and Hebrew readers would have immediately made the connection and understood the imagery.

The thanksgiving offering of the Old Testament, unlike many of the other offerings, could be made at places other than the temple. Part of the thanksgiving offering would be lifted high towards God in the sight of all (Lev 7:14). The person offering the sacrifice had to be ritually clean. This was so important that God declared that if a ritually unclean person ate of the thanksgiving offering "[that person] will be cut off from the community" (Leviticus 7:21).

The imagery is extremely powerful to the Christian. To offer the thanksgiving sacrifice unto God, the royal priest must be ritually clean; he must be washed in the blood of Jesus Christ and stand in his righteousness. No other preparation is acceptable before God.

Oil represents the Holy Spirit, so we need his active presence, anointing, and direction in the thanksgiving sacrifice. Unleavened bread speaks of the things that are untainted by sin, while leavened bread speaks of the imperfect. As redeemed ones, the royal priests have untainted things to offer. As persons still not yet perfected, God indicates his willingness to accept the thanksgiving sacrifice, though parts of us, and so the sacrifice, are imperfect. The thanksgiving sacrifice can be offered up to God anywhere. Parts of the sacrifice may be intensely personal and private, but God expects that parts will be lifted as a wave (or heave) offering that all may see.

Through the prophet Isaiah, God declared, "[I bring] words of praise to their lips" (Isa 57:19). Every Hebrew reader would have understood the sacrificing of fruits and produce unto God in recognition of his sovereignty and blessing, especially the offering of first fruits. Here the writer of Hebrews implies the sacred obligation of the royal priest to offer God the fruit of his lips, as God had, himself, created that fruit, and we make the thanksgiving sacrifice in acknowledgment of his lordship and sovereignty.

Paul writes to the Christians at Colossae that we are to abound in the faith with thanksgiving (Col 2:7). Paul urges the believers to "devote yourselves to prayer with an alert mind and a thankful heart" (Col 4:2). He also counsels the Christians in Philippi, "Don't worry about anything; instead, pray about everything. Tell God what you need, and thank him for all he has done" (Phil 4:6). The thanksgiving sacrifice is no trivial matter, but a part of the daily existence of each royal priest.

A third sacrifice to be made by royal priests is the sacrifice of doing "good and to share" (Heb 13:16). There is no question that people cannot be saved by doing good works (Eph 2:8–9). That is fundamental to Christian belief and practice. Yet, "we are God's masterpiece. He has created us anew in Christ Jesus, so we can do the good things he planned for us long ago" (Eph 2:10).

Bringing to God the sacrifice of good works is something for which the royal priest was created. It is as natural to the Christian as water is to a duck. Since we have been "created in Christ Jesus for good works" we find incredible personal growth and satisfaction in fulfilling our creation mandate.

In the days just before his crucifixion, known today as Holy Week, Jesus taught that the sacrifice of good deeds, even if it be to the simplest person, would be considered, by him, that "you were doing it to me!" (Matt 25:40), and to refuse to offer the sacrifice of good works to even the humblest of all would be that "you were refusing to help me" (Matt 25:45).

In the Sermon on the Mount, considered today as one of the greatest orations of all time, Jesus taught, "I say, love your enemies! Pray for those who persecute you! In that way, you will be acting as true children of your Father in heaven" (Matt 5:44–45). Paul elucidates, "Whenever we have opportunity, we should do good to everyone" (Gal 6:10).

James encapsulates the fundamental nature of good works to the Christian when he declares:

> So you see, faith by itself isn't enough. Unless it produces good deeds, it is dead and useless. Now someone may argue, 'Some people have faith; others have good deeds.' But I say, How can you show me your faith if you don't have good deeds? I will show you my faith by my good deeds. You say you have faith, for you believe that there is one God. Good for you! Even the demons believe this, and they tremble in terror. How foolish! Can't you see that faith without good deeds is useless? (Jas 2:17–20)

Created in Christ to do good works, demonstrating the reality of our faith through good works, seizing every opportunity to do good works, in all this we offer the royal priest's sacrifice to our God. As the life of faith pleases God (Heb 11:6), so the sacrifices of praise and practical ministry give him pleasure.

Writing to Titus, a gentile and fellow minister, Paul urges, "I want you to insist on these teachings so that all who trust in God will devote themselves to doing good. These teachings are good and beneficial for everyone" (Titus 3:8). A few verses later, Paul reiterates the exhortation that "our people must learn to do good" (Titus 3:14).

What would be good works? A wealthy billionaire would be doing good works when he contributes millions of dollars to build a hospital, to send food and personal care items to places like Haiti. To many of us with far fewer funds, good work would include something as simple as sharing a meal with someone less fortunate. Essentially, it is bound in the concepts of servanthood and serving taught by Jesus and expressed in the culture in which the Christian lives.

A fourth sacrifice that the royal priest offers is money, described by Paul as "a sweet-smelling sacrifice that is acceptable and pleasing to God" (Phil 4:18). In terms of the sweet-smelling aroma of a sacrifice, it has been described as representing humans in perfect obedience, yielding to God an offering which is pleasing to him.

Regretfully, some have pushed biblical teaching to an extreme where it begins to sound like capitalistic materialism loosely clothed in religious language. Yet that should not deter the royal priest from understanding and embracing biblical principles of sacrificial giving. Giving and receiving are clearly taught in Scripture. Jesus himself said, "Give, and you will receive. Your gift will return to you in full—pressed down, shaken together to make room for more, running over, and poured into your lap. The amount you give will determine the amount you get back" (Luke 6:38). At the same time, he warns about the reality that money can become a master and that no individual can serve two masters (Matt 6:24; Luke 16:13), and Paul adds that "the love of money is the root of all kinds of evil" (1 Tim 6:10).

Ephesians 4:28 carries an important principle. "If you are a thief, quite stealing. Instead, use your hands for good hard work, and then give generously to others in need" (NLT). This principle establishes that one of the key reasons for earning money is to have the ability to give to those who are in need and not just for the sake of accumulating things or for the material prosperity of the earner.

Christians give sacrificially for the propagation of the gospel, but they also give sacrificially to those who are in need. This is linked very closely with the sacrifice of "doing good and to share."

In discussing the question of who is wealthy, some rabbis quote ancient Jewish sources in defining it as one who is happy with what he has.[4] The child of God learns how to "live on almost nothing or with everything" (Phil 4:12). In each economic circumstance the royal priest can "do everything through Christ who gives me strength" (Phil 4:13). In all conditions the royal priest can offer God the sweet-smelling aroma of sacrificial giving to God's work and to those in need.

A fifth sacrifice that the royal priest offers to God is the "broken spirit" and "a broken and a repentant heart" (Ps 51:17). Psalm 51 records David's agonizing prayer of repentance when the prophet Nathan confronted him about his adultery with Bathsheba and his subsequent murder of her husband, Uriah. Nathan's words helped David to see his sin as God saw it, and when we see our sin in that light it breaks the heart and the spirit.

How far have we drifted away from God when sin becomes just a little sex? When sin is minimized, rationalized, and excused, the Spirit of God mourns as he is thrust to the margins of our lives. Oh, that God would break our hearts by letting us glimpse how he sees the sin we have embraced! In that awful reality we find the grace of God. In finding the grace of God and the forgiveness of the cross of Jesus, we discover the purging of sin, the washing of the spirit, the creation of a clean heart and the renewal of a steadfast spirit.

Being a royal priest in God's kingdom is an incredible privilege. With the position comes the responsibility to mediate and to offer sacrifices. May every child of God embrace his or her position in Christ, exercise his or her privileges, and fulfill his or her responsibilities that societies may be transformed, and the fragrance of Christ be known throughout the entire world (2 Cor 2:15–16).

---

4. Telushkin, *Jewish Values*, 95.

PENETRATING SOCIETY

When the benediction is pronounced as we close our time assembled, we begin leaving the building, or place where we assembled, and become distributed throughout society. For every one of us, it is then that a major part of our ministry begins. If we are all priests, then we all have a ministry to carry out during the time we are distributed, penetrating the society. Every Christian is a priest, and every priest has a ministry.

Regretfully, we have allowed a perception to develop whereby ministry takes place only when we are assembled and, then, by the few while the many sit passively and watch. This is wrong on every level.

It is time to recapture the principle of ministry throughout all aspects of our lives. Every vocation is to come under the lordship of Jesus. Every profession provides significant ministry in the wider community and throughout the country. Do not limit God to a few short hours on a Sunday morning. Understand that he has placed us where he wants us to be so that we can function as the Church right where we are.

The principle enunciated by the apostle Paul is "work with enthusiasm, as though you were working for the Lord rather than for people" (Eph 6:7). Work is, itself, ministry and can be amazingly effective in sharing the principles of the kingdom of God and bringing the supernatural into the natural, where Christians outside the Church can be significantly impactful. This is where ministry expands and is built outside the walls of the church building, in the place where God has planted Christians vocationally or professionally for the time being.

The very essence of being salt and light (Matt 5:13–16) is when Christians are distributed through the wider community so that the salt and light of our presence and our spiritual reality comes into direct contact with people who are living in disobedience to God without the expectation of eternal life. That salt and light is manifested daily through our jobs and professions, in the excellence of our work and in the integrity we display in our everyday lives, in our place of employment, in our communities, our homes, and in our servanthood.

Sally was acting in a temporary post of an educational organization. When the board of the organization was discussing permanently appointing Sally, her immediate supervisor gave her a glowing recommendation: always arriving on time, working late, meeting deadlines on time, excellent performance in her duties. On that recommendation the board appointed her to the post. One year later, when reviewing Sally's performance, the supervisor noted that, since her appointment, Sally rarely worked late, she missed important deadlines, her work standards had dropped, and she had informed everyone that her church "came first" and nothing would be allowed to keep her from "her church."

Sally's testimony was shattered by her attitude and any light she brought to that institution was effectively snuffed out, and her salt totally lost its savor. Sally made the common mistake of seeing ministry only in terms of what took place within the four walls of the church building for very few hours a week and failed to understand that her greatest ministry, over numerous hours weekly, was in the institution where God had placed her to impact the staff and students at every level. To effectively accomplish her main ministry, she needed to be salt and light in her attitude, her work ethic, and her relationships with others within the educational institution where she worked Monday to Friday.

The pastor of a congregation within the official church in China, where evangelism is against the law, was asked how was it that he reported baptizing some three hundred new converts annually and having a growing congregation in the thousands. He replied that he taught people to live like Jesus so that friends and colleagues could enquire why they lived by such different principles and their lives seemed so different. Once asked, they were legally free to share why they were different from the people around them. In so doing, every Christian was exercising the ministry God had given them in the place where they had been assigned by God.

When we understand the Church is to be a community of priests, we begin to grasp the reality that our distribution through society allows the Church to directly impact every aspect of that society through our vocations, which are the ministries God has entrusted to us.

God has placed us in the professions, vocations, and businesses where he wants us. Are we willing to function under the Holy Spirit's anointing and direction to be and do what God wants us to be and do where he has placed us? It is critical that each committed Christian understands calling or vocation to be a ministry given for each person to uniquely impact the society as a royal priest. The divide of vocations considered sacred and those considered secular that dominated theological thinking for most of the twentieth century, may in fact be a false divide not really supported by God and the Scriptures.

If we are each a royal priest regardless of gender, race, education, or social class, then:

1. Every Christian is in ministry regardless of the level and arena in which he/she may individually serve.

2. The sacred-secular divide may indeed be false. If Col 1:15–20 is taken seriously then this divide is, indeed, artificial, for God's Word declares that "through him [Jesus] God created everything," and that "he holds all creation together," and "so he is first in everything," and finally, "through him God reconciled everything to himself." If the words "all" and "everything" mean what they say, then every aspect of our lives and societies needs to come under the lordship of Jesus.

3. Consequently, every vocation can be transformational and is intended to be a means of bringing God's glory and lordship to some aspect of his creation until "the whole earth is full of his glory!" (Isa 6:3).

4. Regardless of profession or job, we are royal priests intended to bring his glory to every corner of society. So, fulfill your destiny in Christ. Bring every avenue of life and every aspect of society under his lordship.

We have endangered the ministry by confining it, by example and in teaching, to what goes on behind the pulpits and on the platforms of our church buildings. Is not the ministry exercised when the priest of God works in the corporate board room to make a difference, in the government's civil service, in the legal profession, in the schools, in the hospitals, in the offices and shops, in our homes, and on our streets to minister biblical principles through the grace and mercy of God, to bless and change lives through the power of cleansing in the shed blood of Jesus Christ, and thereby change situations?

Why have we confined ministry to buildings and scheduled services and, increasingly, just to that time when people come to the altar towards the end of a service, when we agree that the Church is clearly neither the building nor the program and when ministry is, obviously, intended to be the life-consuming force of every believer in every situation and profession where he or she has been placed by God?

The Hebrew word *avodah*, in the Scriptures, means worship and work. Work, if done unto God with integrity, is a recognized form of worship in the Jewish context. There has never been a concept of distinguishing our work from our life of faith in the Bible. It must be clear that Christians understand that doing the work they are employed to do is ministry that brings salt, light, and leaven in the workplace. God expects each of us to use our total life experience as ministry to further his kingdom around the earth.

Have we evangelicals unwittingly embraced the division of clergy and laity and, for far too long, limited ministry to the role of the pastor in a congregation? I well remember, in 1980, when I returned to Barbados from Dominica and took the position of manager of a Christian bookstore rather than a pastorate, that a dear pastor-friend asked me very seriously why I had left the ministry. I burst out laughing. We continue to hold onto this erroneous, unbiblical concept that only a few of us who function as pastors are in ministry and the rest are laity. We are all in ministry where God has placed us.

All work has dignity as an expression of the creativity of the divine image in which mankind has been made. There is a divine calling upon us to bring out that inherent creativity in the place where God has put us to minister as light and salt to the generation in which we serve. "Whatever you do, do it all for the glory of God" (1 Cor 10:31).

The greatest facet of ministry is not in the pulpit, though the pulpit is vital to the organism that is the Church. The greatest facet of ministry is the application of salt and light in our daily lives right where God has placed us to demonstrate the power of God and the reality of his presence.

As Moses set apart Aaron and his sons for the Levitical priesthood (Lev 8:12–35), he anointed the lobes of the right ear, right thumb, and right big toe. This defined the importance of their service in hearing God through his Holy Spirit and the Scriptures (which had not yet been compiled in its current format), the importance of their servanthood to God and their fellow humans, and the importance of walking (i.e., living) in obedience to God.

May the royal priests of the twenty-first century understand and live out these realities wherever they have been placed by God in the society in which they live.

CHAPTER 9

Holy Nation

PETER TAKES THE CONCEPT of being a holy nation that was first ascribed to Israel (Exod 19:6), and applies it to the Church (1 Pet 2:9). It is not that the Church is replacing Israel in the plan of God, but that the Church is being grafted into and, in part, fulfilling the promise that God made to Israel as the Jews emerged from slavery in Egypt to form their own nation, and his promise to Abraham that, through him, all the families on earth would be blessed (Gen 12:3).

ISRAEL AS HOLY NATION

As Israel departed from Egypt they were embarking on a completely new experience. Israel entered Egypt as a large and wealthy family. During the four centuries of sojourn in Egypt, they developed into hundreds of thousands of people who maintained their distinctive identity without being assimilated into the culture and national ethos of Egypt, despite being eventually enslaved. When they left Egypt, it was to form a separate, sovereign nation for the first time.

Standing on the threshold of this new experience, God declares Israel a holy nation. Much needed to be done to become a nation. For example, they would need land and societal structures. God's promise to Abraham included the land of Canaan. It would eventually take another forty years after their exodus from Egypt for this promise to begin to become a reality and, even then, would require many battles to realistically possess the land. In the meantime, Israel would be a theocracy where God would rule first through Moses, then Joshua, and then through the judges and prophets until the people rejected theocracy in favor of monarchy, and God gave them Saul as their king.

Societal structures would also take time to build. In Exodus through to Deuteronomy, Moses, in conversation with God, begins to lay the foundation for the structures needed to build a nation. Among these, the instructions for religious concepts were laid out. A priestly caste was consecrated, and a tabernacle built to house the actual furniture and vessels to be used in worship. This enabled the culture of the new nation of Israel to begin to take shape, a culture that would, in many ways, be radically different from the surrounding nations.

In the tabernacle, God would commune with Moses and, then, the high priests of succeeding generations. The laws laid out the societal structure for worshiping God.

A system of justice was devised to provide a series of adjudicators to settle disputes (Exod 18:13–27), and provision was made when the Israelites settled in Canaan to set aside specific cities as places of refuge (Num 35:9–34), especially for persons accused of murder. It would take time to build these and other societal structures, and the record of the Old Testament's historical books give some insight into how these structures were developed, used, and sometimes, misused or ignored.

Other structures included the beginnings of a welfare system as provision was made for widows and orphans to be able to glean in the fields after the harvests were collected, with the corners being left specifically for them. An interesting system of land ownership was also instituted where land could be sold, but, in the Year of Jubilee, was to be returned to the original owner or a direct heir. Additionally, the nearest relative could buy back the land as the "kinsman redeemer." This gave a family that had gone through economic challenges the opportunity to move out of absolute poverty back into land ownership.

Above everything else, Israel was to be an example of how God would deal with the nations and the benefits of serving YHWH, above all others, as the one true God. As fallen human beings, Israel was not always a good example, and there were times when God had to raise up another nation to bring Israel back to their rightful place, through military defeat and subjugation, by a nation the Israelis would consider heathen. The small book of Habakkuk is an example of this reality as the prophet Habakkuk engages God in a discussion of this very matter.

CHURCH AS NATION

By joining the Church to Israel as a holy nation, Peter extends the concept of nation to embrace something that really is not a nation in the conventional understanding of the term. It must be noted here that Peter is not teaching that the Church replaces Israel, as that nation still features prominently in God's prophetic agenda. The Church is grafted into the metaphor of a nation, demonstrating the visible reality of God's dealing with humanity in the world.

As the citizens of Israel were brought out of slavery in Egypt, so the members of the Church are brought out of the bondage and dominance of sin to a new reality of existence. As Israel had foundational written principles and precepts on which it built its national culture, the Church has many of the same written precepts and principles on which is founded its unique culture, which is able to penetrate and positively transform any national culture within which it is planted.

As the nation of Israel entered into a blood covenant with God, the strongest type of covenant in the ancient world—established initially between God and Abraham (Gen 15:8–21) and solidified in the blood sacrifices of the tabernacle and, subsequently, the temple—so the Church is in a blood covenant with God, established between God and man through the sacrifice of Christ on the cross and his subsequent resurrection.

The most significant aspect of the Church as nation is in the reality of the example it presents of the rule of God. The Church, with all its foibles, remains the only current representation on earth of what the kingdom of God would look like. In the Church, people everywhere have an opportunity to see the actuality of the rule of God in the lives of individuals and societies as the covenant with God and the culture of the Church take root and deepen, as expressed in the Scripture lived out by Jesus' disciples in practical, life-transforming terms.

The Church is intended to be the physical manifestation for the gospel, set forth in tangible terms for the world to see and understand. In this way, it is a "nation" among the nations of the world, unique and visible. "God's purpose in all this was to use the church to display his wisdom in its rich variety to all the unseen rulers and authorities in the heavenly places. This was his eternal plan, which he carried out through Christ Jesus our Lord" (Eph 3:10–11).

If the Church as "nation" is removed from society, the visible representation of the gospel is also removed. There are countries where the organized church is repressed and persecuted. Nevertheless, while the organization might be repressed, the organism remains vibrant and alive and demonstrates the gospel visibly through lifestyles that reflect God at every level.

When organization subsumes organism in the expression of the Church, it becomes easier for the Church itself to be conformed to the surrounding culture of the society where it resides. Once that happens the Church loses its uniqueness as "nation" and becomes a social club to perpetuate existing societal norms rather than a radical revolution that transforms lives and cultural customs.

CHURCH AS HOLY NATION

The Church is not just a nation, but is a holy nation.

One use of the word "holy" in Scripture is the concept of being set apart unto God. As holy nation, the Church is set apart for

God. This is not separationist in that the Church is to remove its involvement in the world, but the concept that it is different from the world in which it serves and, essentially, sets forth the presence of God in society being set apart for him. In the prayer Jesus prayed the night of his betrayal, John records that Jesus prayed to God the Father, "I'm not asking you to take them out of the world, but to keep them safe from the evil one" (John 17:15).

Such a separation as holy nation involves moving from a lifestyle of disobedience to a lifestyle of obedience to God. This is a move away from identifying with evil towards associating with that which is true, honorable, right, pure, lovely, and admirable (Phil 4:8). It is a positive projection of the culture of God's kingdom among humans rather than a negative connotation of cutting off interaction with the surrounding world. It is, ultimately, separation to God exclusively, set apart to preserve the knowledge and worship of God in the world.

The word "holy" also carries the meaning of moral purity (1 Pet 1:15–16). It is intended that the nation of Israel and the Church be communities where moral purity is practiced and where others can see the benefits of that pure relationship with God expressed in day-to-day living.

The on-the-ground reality is that both the nation of Israel and the Church are made up of flawed human beings who, too often, embrace disobedience and sin rather than moral purity. This raises the question as to whether the Church and Israel have failed in their mission to be "holy nation." There is moral failure among broken human beings, even those in Israel and the Church, as history clearly testifies. This moral failure draws everyone's attention to the ideal that God desires, and should serve to draw those of us in the Church deeper into God's grace and the transforming power of the Holy Spirit through the shed blood of Jesus Christ.

When Christians live in the reality of being holy nation, life takes on deeper purpose and meaning. If Christians are the visible representation of the gospel, then every aspect of life is meaningful. In our homes, businesses, vocations, and professions we present the visible reality of God, his word, and the gospel. It is the

Church distributed widely through society that demonstrates the example of holy nation to the world, not the Church assembled behind its walls and closed, or even open, doors.

As Paul puts it in Col 3:12, "Since God chose you to be the holy people he loves, you must clothe yourselves with tender-hearted mercy, kindness, humility, gentleness, and patience." These visibly portray core values of the Church's culture that disciples can exemplify when they are distributed throughout the community.

CHAPTER 10

Lifestyle Generosity

THE GOD WHOM WE serve is an incredibly generous God. This is epitomized in the well-known verse John 3:16, "God loved the world so much that he gave . . ." Through the crucifixion of Jesus, we can experience the generosity of God expressed in grace, mercy, and compassion. Reflecting God to the people around us must include his likeness of generosity as part of our lifestyle. Our generosity reflects the grace and goodness of God expressed in practical terms in a society where individual rights and privileges seem to trump everything else. It is also a reflection of our servanthood as we serve generously in every way.

Jesus was exceedingly generous while he was on earth. He healed the sick, raised the dead, fed thousands at one meal, and turned water into wine at a wedding feast. His generosity was expressed through his disciples as he sent them out to "heal the sick, raise the dead, cure those with leprosy, and cast out demons. Give as freely as you have received!" (Matt 10:8). That last sentence emphasizes that Christian disciples freely receive much from God. That level of generosity then sets the motivation and pattern for our generous lifestyles. The context in this passage is clearly about spiritual realities and not just about money.

The Bible frequently urges readers to be generous. For example, Prov 11:24–25 exhorts us to "give freely and become more wealthy; be stingy and lose everything. The generous will prosper;

those who refresh others will themselves be refreshed." These verses are not in the context of giving to a local church or to some big-name preacher. It is in the context of giving to each other within our communities as generously as we have received from God.

Generosity is not the sole preserve of the rich. In fact, many charitable organizations have found that it is the mass of small monetary donations, not the big checks, that enable them to carry out their mandates. Paul says of the Macedonian Christians, "They are being tested by many troubles, and they are very poor. But they are also filled with abundant joy, which has overflowed in rich generosity" (2 Cor 8:2). "Very poor" but overflowing "in rich generosity." To our twenty-first-century mindset, this seems to be a contradiction in terms, perhaps part of the enigma of the Church. Yet it is as true today as when the apostle Paul wrote it more than 1,900 years ago.

Jesus, standing and watching people make their financial contributions to the temple, noticed a woman give two of the smallest coins available at the time. Her gift was noticed because it represented all the money she had (Mark 12:44). She gave out of her poverty, not out of her wealth. Generosity is a lifestyle for all economic brackets in society.

Generosity, itself, is not primarily about money but is about a condition of the heart, a lifestyle, a reflection of the God we love and serve, and involves much more than just the money that may be available. It is possible to be generous with time in several ways, giving time to be with the lonely or to a child who needs the presence of a mature person who cares. Words can be used generously to encourage and motivate. There are so many other ways to be generous when the heart is filled with God's love, joy, and generosity.

In encouraging the Corinthians to give generously to the relief fund they were collecting for the Christians in Jerusalem, who were experiencing severe deprivation, Paul laid down two important principles, "Yes, you will be enriched in every way so that you can always be generous. And when we take your gifts to those who need them, they will thank God" (2 Cor 9:11). Usually, though we could always find exceptions, God enriches the generous so they can be more generous, and the recipients of genuine generosity are moved to give thanks to God as they become aware of his reflection in that generosity.

Only what is given away can be enriched and multiplied back to the giver. Indeed, "Blessed are those who are generous" (Prov 22:9). It is a biblical principle that we always receive back more than we give (Luke 6:38).

Reiterating, the context of giving in 2 Cor 8–9 is that of Christians giving to other people who are in need. The context is not giving to support the local congregation. Read those chapters again. It is crystal clear. Unfortunately, our leaders have too often couched their teaching on generosity as though it only means persons giving to the local church or ministry, and seldom teach us that our generosity goes much further as we give freely to those around us who are in need.

Apostle Paul had some interesting instructions for those who were thieves. "If you are a thief, quit stealing. Instead, use your hands for good hard work, and then give generously to others in need" (Eph 4:28). So, the instruction was not to work to accumulate, but to work to have something to give so that generosity becomes a reality in the former thief's transformed life. The thief is moved from a selfish lifestyle that takes from others to a generous lifestyle that gives to others. A radical turn in the opposite direction.

In correlation, for centuries Judaism's traditions have insisted on generosity. In fact, not being generous is seen as idolatry and generosity is often equated with justice in Jewish teaching.[1] Jews have been taught for centuries that children are born selfish and must be taught to be generous. Our children need to be taught how to be generous so that generosity becomes their lifestyles as they grow older.

God can, and will, lead us in the expression of his generosity in a needy world. If we are born again believers, we can expect to be prompted by the Holy Spirit in all areas of our lives, even

---

1. Telushkin, *Jewish Wisdom*, 16.

in how to exercise our generosity. Sadly, there are many people seeking to scam naive Christians out of their money and belongings. It is, therefore, helpful to be open to the inner promptings of the Holy Spirit in how to exercise our generosity in simple and profound ways that express God's generosity. This kind of generosity is the practical outworking of the Church within every stratum of society, distributing the generosity of God so that he would be glorified. As Ps 37:21 says, "The godly are generous givers."

Tim was on his way home. As he slowed to turn into the avenue that would take him to his home, he noticed a man walking into the same avenue. Immediately he sensed in his spirit that he was to give this man twenty dollars. At first Tim resisted. It seemed such a silly thing to do. However, Tim stopped his car next to the man and handed him the twenty dollars, saying that he just felt he was to give him the money. The man's eyes filled with tears as he took the twenty-dollar bill. Tim drove off as he felt the specific need in this man's life was not his business. He was simply being the generosity of God in a moment of human need.

Pastor Will was standing in the church yard. He noticed an individual walking straight towards him. He also heard the word "no" very loudly in his spirit. As this person reached Pastor Will, he began asking for thousands of dollars, but the negative word in his spirit was enough to stop Pastor Will from giving anything on that occasion. Real generosity comes from deep within, where the Holy Spirit can be a guide.

An elderly lady, with a foreign accent, was buying a few items at the supermarket. The cashier loudly told her the money she had received from the woman was insufficient to cover the cost of the few items she was buying. Seeing the woman's embarrassment at not having any more money, Russell, who was next in line, leaned over and, on finding out the amount needed was less than twenty dollars, he paid the bill, enabling the woman to get her small number of groceries and eliminating much of the embarrassment. Russell never introduced himself to the woman as, for him, a random act of kindness simply reflected the grace and compassion of God in his own life.

In the Caribbean island of Barbados, there are many stories of women who did not have much. Invariably, they grew much of the food they ate in their own kitchen gardens. Yet everyone in the neighborhood knew they could go to that person's home and be served a hot meal whenever needed. Most of these women were committed Christians reflecting the generosity of God with what they had, sometimes in very difficult circumstances. God saw to it that there was always food in their pots and love in their hearts and homes.

Rebekah (Gen 24:46) is a biblical example of generosity. Asked for a drink of water, she willingly gave it to Abraham's servant, a total stranger to her. Then, unbidden, she poured water for his camels to drink, willingly making more than one trip to the well to fetch sufficient water for the thirsty camels.

An example of a simple gift is found in John 6:5–13. A young boy has only five small barley loaves and two fish for his own lunch. By giving them to Jesus, that small gift was miraculously transformed into enough food to feed thousands. Never think a gift is too small when it is given in obedience to God's word and the promptings of the Holy Spirit.

One of the best-known stories of generosity in the Bible is the parable Jesus told of the good Samaritan (Luke 10:29–37). The parable tells of a Jew waylaid and brutalized by robbers and left bleeding and injured beside the road. Jewish officials passed by on the other side of the road. A Samaritan, a member of a group despised by Jews, stopped to help. He bound the man's wounds and took him to a place of safety. Jesus used the parable to illustrate that those in need are our neighbors, who we should help in those times of need, regardless of them being socially acceptable or not.

One of the names of our God in the Jewish Scriptures is El Shaddai. Literally translated, it means "God of more than enough." Our God is an abundant provider in all spheres of life. It is possible for poverty to become an ingrained mindset, which causes us to miss the generosity of God and the expression of his generosity through our lives. When we understand who is our source, it changes our mindset. This enables us to develop the lifestyle of generosity, understanding that it is not dependent on our circumstances but on the El Shaddai, the God who is more than enough.

Regretfully, too many define themselves by the possession of material things instead of by the grace and generosity of the God they serve. That inevitably leads to selfishness. In many ways our generosity, or lack thereof, reflects what we really think about God. In Jesus' teaching in Matt 25:31–46, he makes it clear that generosity is not a suggestion, or even just an option, but is an expected outcome of a life lived in relationship with him.

In understanding the God who is more than enough, we begin to see that one of the ways deep-rooted spirituality is expressed practically in society is through a lifestyle of generosity. Generosity demonstrates the grace of God in our lives and, as we are all growing in grace, we will all be at different stages of our journey. Yet the inner reality of God's generous grace flows out through our own generosity to those around us. Consequently, generosity is a practical expression of the gospel.

James is quite pointed about generosity, or "good deeds," in his epistle (2:14–20). He is adamant "that faith without good deeds is useless." Generosity to others is a clear proof and demonstration of love for God. Generosity is also an investment in eternity and the primary way we accumulate wealth in the kingdom of heaven (Matt 6:19–20).

Given that in the first century the Church was totally organism and the organization and institution had not developed much, very little is said in the New Testament about giving to support the administration of the Church. Congregations met in homes so there were no utility bills and building upkeep costs. There were few in the way of formal, full-time clergy and, so, no monthly salaries were needed. It is clear in Paul's writings that some congregations gave to him, thereby enabling him to minister to others. Yet at times he worked at a trade to take care of his own financial needs.

In the Old Testament God's method of supporting the Levites, who were the full-time priests of that period, was through the tithes and offerings of the people. Jesus endorses this system in

Matt 23:23, "You should tithe, yes, but do not neglect the more important things." It is one of the fairest ways of providing for the upkeep of the institutional and organizational aspects of the Church. However, it should never become a legalistic requirement, but should be a celebration of love between God and his children. Through tithing we return to God out of his generous supply to us and he commits himself to be even more generous towards us. Tithing is one of the best arrangements there can be; for, when God needs ten dollars he gives us one hundred dollars, we return to him the ten dollars and get to keep the change.

Jesus is quite clear in his teaching that you cannot be a servant of God and a servant of money (Matt 6:24) at the same time, for no one can serve two masters. Sir Winston Churchill, whose witticisms are often quoted, is said to have declared that generosity is always wise.[2]

Greed is the very antithesis of generosity, as it expresses selfishness and does not reflect the nature of our God, the El Shaddai. Sadly, greed is too often found among Christians and Christian leaders and, regretfully, has even become spiritualized in some cases.

In the final analysis, all that we have comes from God, "Remember the Lord your God. He is the one who gives you power to be successful" (Deut 8:18). Proverbs 10:22 also states, "The blessing of the Lord makes a person rich, and he adds no sorrow with it." Through the prophet Hosea, God says of Israel, "She doesn't realize it was I who gave her everything she has—the grain, the new wine, the olive oil; I even gave her silver and gold" (Hos 2:8). When we remember he is our generous provider, we can develop a lifestyle of generosity that impacts the people around us.

On a final note concerning generosity, Jesus made it clear that when we express generosity in our everyday lives, we are to do so anonymously. "Give your gifts in private, and your Father, who sees everything, will reward you" (Matt 6:4).

---

2. Humes, *Wit and Wisdom*, 41.

CHAPTER 11

Empowered

WHEN JESUS GAVE INSTRUCTIONS to his disciples (Matt 28:18–20) on their task in the years ahead of them, he also gave them the promise that God the Holy Spirit would be sent to lead them into truth (John 14:17), and teach them and remind them of Jesus' teaching (John 14:26). Jesus also promised that this same Holy Spirit would give the disciples power, specifically in the context of witnessing to the truth of the gospel.

In his first epistle to the congregations in Corinth, Paul reminds the Corinthian Christians that, when he took the gospel to that city, "Rather than using clever and persuasive speeches, I relied only on the power of the Holy Spirit" (1 Cor 2:4). That "power of the Holy Spirit" is clear throughout the book of Acts in the Bible.

The Church was born in the power of the Holy Spirit. There is no indication that this power was only for a few short years and would then be withdrawn. In fact, it could be reasonably argued that the twenty-first century needs at least as much power and demonstration of the Holy Spirit as the first century. As stated in Acts 1:8, "But you will receive power when the Holy Spirit comes upon you. And you will be my witnesses, telling people about me everywhere—in Jerusalem, throughout Judea, in Samaria, and to the ends of the earth."

In his final moments with his disciples prior to his ascension into the heavenlies, Jesus did not give them a strategic plan or detailed program for the development of the Church under his new covenant. Rather, in this time of leadership transition, Jesus told these disciples, about 120 in number, to go into Jerusalem, just across the Kidron Valley from the Mount of Olives where they were standing, and await the Holy Spirit who would give them power to be witnesses "in Jerusalem, throughout Judea, in Samaria, and to the ends of the earth."

The Greek word that Scripture records that Jesus used for "power" is the word *dynamis* (or *dunamis,* as in some commentaries), from which we derive the English words dynamite and dynamo. This conveys the idea of significant power. Robinson and Wall define *dynamis* as a power that can be demonstrated and felt, a power that enables the carrying out of the Church's God-given mission.[1] Bullinger translates the word as "power in action."[2] This is not authority, nor is it clever oratory that persuades individuals to embrace Christ as their Savior. Paul gives us some insight when he reminds the Christians in Corinth that "my message and my preaching were very plain. Rather than using clever and persuasive speeches, I relied only on the power of the Holy Spirit." Even a cursory reading of the book of Acts in the New Testament shows that Paul demonstrated this power generated by the Holy Spirit in miraculous deeds that attested to the truth and power of the gospel he preached.

Second Timothy 1:7 states, "For God has not given us a spirit of fear and timidity, but of power, love, and self-discipline." This verse is not often considered when reflecting on the power granted to those who are disciples of Jesus Christ. The Greek word used here for "given" means to give freely, to supply. So, this is referring to something God has specifically given and continues to freely supply to Christians.

Once again, the Greek word for "power" in 2 Tim 1:7 is *dynamis*, with all that word implies, as described above. The context in which this power is released to Christians is love and self-discipline,

---

1. Robinson and Wall, *Called*, 34.
2. Bullinger, *Concordance*, 598.

the very same context in which the operational power of the Holy Spirit is described in 1 Cor 12–14.

From these two passages of Scripture, it is truly clear that the Church, the people who are disciples of Jesus, is intended, through God's gift, to be spiritually powerful in the world that was then, and still is now, under the dominion of a spiritual power, which is in rebellion against God. This God-given power, it must be reiterated, is exercised in love and self-discipline.

A critical passage in this discussion is 1 Cor 12:7–11:

> A spiritual gift is given to each of us so we can help each other. To one person the Spirit gives the ability to give wise advice; to another the same Spirit gives a message of special knowledge. The same Spirit gives great faith to another, and to someone else the one Spirit gives the gift of healing. He gives one person the power to perform miracles, and another the ability to prophesy. He gives someone else the ability to discern whether a message is from the Spirit of God or from another spirit. Still another person is given the ability to speak in unknown languages, while another is given the ability to interpret what is being said. It is the one and only Spirit who distributes all these gifts. He alone decides which gift each person should have.

First Corinthians 12 through 14 set a context for the demonstration of these power gifts.

Paul carefully emphasizes that these are gifts from the Holy Spirit, and he alone decides who receives them. It is the Holy Spirit who incarnates these power gifts through the lives of believers. They are gifts given by the grace of God through the agency of the Holy Spirit. They are not intended to aggrandize the individual through whom the gift is demonstrated. It is all the Holy Spirit and no one else. These are supernatural gifts, nothing is dependent on human ability, natural talent, or education. They are expressed in a moment when the Holy Spirit manifests his specific power through an individual Christian and then that moment is finished.

Here are the nine gifts outlined in 1 Cor 12 and their application in a human context of the Church distributed throughout society.

WISE ADVICE

In some English translations this is rendered as a "word of wisdom." This is a message spoken audibly for the benefit of others. It is not enhanced human preparation or even commonsense. It goes beyond human wisdom. Being a gift from the Holy Spirit, this wisdom is a supernatural message taken from the wisdom of God and given to a specific person in order that a specific need would be resolved at a specific point in time. Many theologians limit their understanding of this gift to supernatural insight into a particular problem or need with the application of Scripture to that explicit issue. It may not be necessary to limit this gift in this way as the divine wisdom of the Holy Spirit can be applicable in a multitude of areas but will never contradict the Scriptures in any way.

Acts 10:9–21 is an example of the wise advice the Holy Spirit gave the apostle Peter as he was about to open the door to the gentiles to enter God's kingdom as expressed through the Church. It could, therefore, be described as timely supernatural insight that is directive.

Oliver heads a government department on a Caribbean island. The small island nation was facing a significant issue that would negatively impact its ability to function in the international business arena. Oliver was also an intercessor. In prayer, a solution to the issue came to mind. Oliver called the prime minister, and the solution was promptly initiated with tangible benefits to that small Caribbean nation—wise advice directed by the Holy Spirit at a critical moment in the governance of a small-island developing nation.

MESSAGE OF SPECIAL KNOWLEDGE

This is rendered in some translations as a "word of knowledge." This is not knowledge gained by long years of study and experience. It is a supernatural insight provided out of the Holy Spirit's omniscience into a specific situation, of which the bearer of the message could have no knowledge—a fragment of God's infinite knowledge, his omniscience, as it were.

An example of this is found in Acts 5:1–11, when the Holy Spirit revealed to the apostle Peter the deception Ananias and Sapphira had devised with respect to a monetary gift they agreed to donate to the fledging church in Jerusalem. Acts 9:10–12 provides another example where Ananias, a devout Christian leader, later identified in Acts with a prophetic ministry, received specific information about Saul, who we know better as the apostle Paul. Again, in Acts 20:22–23, Paul indicates that he has received special knowledge from the Holy Spirt about his final trip to Jerusalem. Another example is in Acts 27:18–26, when Paul knew that the ship tossed about in a storm would sink but there would be no loss of life.

There are many accounts of Minister Lydia Mings, affectionately known as Mother Mings, being used by the Holy Spirit in the exercise of this gift in congregations, who are members of the Barbados District of the Pentecostal Assemblies of the West Indies, during the first half of the twentieth century. It is said that when congregants heard that Mother Mings would be ministering in their church, everyone would seek the forgiveness of God for any shortcoming or sin in their lives as Mother Mings would be sure to call them out in front of the congregation to repent and set right whatever moral or spiritual wrong she had been told about by the Holy Spirit.

GREAT FAITH

Every believer has faith that they have exercised to become a disciple of Jesus, known as saving faith. This supernatural gift is not general saving faith, nor is it the gradual increase in faith that Christians experience in learning the Scriptures and living out the biblical principles learned. It is a moment when a particle of supernatural faith is imparted to the individual for a definite purpose. It is sometimes referred to as "mountain-moving-faith" (Matt 21:21). It could include an ability to inspire faith in others. It is often accompanied by great boldness.

GIFT OF HEALING

In the Greek, the words for "gift" and "healing" are both in the plural, indicating that there are different gifts that can be exercised under the sovereign direction of the Holy Spirit for the healing of the body, mind, and spirit. Each time the Holy Spirit demonstrates healing in this way, it is a precise gift of healing he has deposited at that moment in the individuals exercising and receiving the gift. It is most often instantaneous and easily visible. As in all other gifts, it is the exercise of the specific power of the Holy Spirit.

Humans, from time to time, need physical, mental, and emotional healing. Some would suggest spiritual healing as well, to recover from the spiritual abuse that is sometimes inflicted by leaders of the disciples of Jesus. Each can be supernaturally healed by a gift of healing effected under the sovereignty of the Holy Spirit. Each healing takes a special gift. The healing of the man at the Golden Gate, also known as the Beautiful Gate, is a clear example of this gift in operation (Acts 3:1–11). Acts 5:15–16 records this gift in operation through the apostle Peter. There are numerous examples of Jesus exercising this gift, as recorded in the Gospels.

POWER TO PERFORM MIRACLES

This is translated in some versions of the Bible as "working of miracles." This too is rendered in the Greek by two plural words indicating that each time one of these miracles is performed it is a unique gift from the Holy Spirit. This is the supernatural power of the Holy Spirit expressed at certain times and would include the casting out of demons, providing protection, and altering circumstances.

Acts 13:9–12 is an example of this gift as Paul responded to Elymas, the sorcerer, and Elymas was struck blind. Paul states in 2 Cor 12:12 that while he was in Corinth, he "did many signs and wonders and miracles." The gift to perform miracles is exemplified in Jesus turning water into wine, feeding thousands with two fish and five small loaves of bread, walking on water, and calming storms instantly.

THE ABILITY TO PROPHESY

These are Holy Spirit inspired, spontaneous, unpremeditated messages spoken audibly in a language known by those present and given at a particular moment in time. It is not so much about foretelling (though that can be included as in Acts 11:28) but more forthtelling the incredible truths of God. The result is that listeners are edified, strengthened in their Christian experience and faith. Acts 2:14–36 is seen as an example of this gift of prophecy.

Prophecy, in this context, is the verbalizing of an insight into a distinctive situation, a message communicated through a disciple of Jesus by the Holy Spirit. The emphasis of these messages is what is important to God. As humans, we are sometimes tempted to insert our own thoughts mingled among the messages from the Holy Spirit. This is one reason why the apostle Paul states, "Let two or three people prophesy, and let the others evaluate what is said" (1 Cor 14:29). Acts 21:8–9 states that Philip the evangelist had four daughters who prophesied. The end of the very first Church Council in Acts 15:32 is noted in this context, "Then Judas and Silas, both being prophets, spoke at length to the believers, encouraging and strengthening their faith." First Corinthians 14:3 explicitly says prophecies strengthen, encourage, and comfort others. It could, therefore, be concluded that this gift is primarily given by the Holy Spirit for the edification of believers in Jesus.

THE ABILITY TO DISCERN WHETHER A MESSAGE IS FROM THE SPIRIT OF GOD OR FROM ANOTHER SPIRIT

This is translated by some English Bibles as "discerning of spirits." Once again, the Greek words are plurals, indicating that these are individual revelations from the Holy Spirit at precise points in time.

There are three types of spirits operational on earth: the Holy Spirit, the human spirit, and the angelic beings, some of whom are in rebellion against God and, so, are considered demonic. This gift enables its user to supernaturally recognize which spirit is motivating speech or behavior at a particular point in time.

A clear example of this is found in Acts 16:16–18, where Paul discerned which spirit was inspiring the words of a young woman, and then Paul was given a gift of working of miracles to cast out the demon that was manifesting through the young woman. Peter also utilized this gift in Acts 8:18–24, when he encountered Simon the sorcerer who wanted to purchase the power of the Holy Spirit. Peter discerned the spiritual condition of the sorcerer and publicly rebuked him. This gift is especially essential for the Church in the twenty-first century, as a variety of spiritual expressions are rampant and seem to be increasing.

Jonathon Cahn, in his book *The Return of the Gods*, lays out a spiritual scenario that has developed in North America, and quite possibly in other countries, where the demonic principalities of the first century AD are returning forcefully in the twenty-first century. In any such reality the ability to discern which spirit is at work in any specific situation is essential to the Church.

THE ABILITY TO SPEAK IN UNKNOWN LANGUAGES

Some English Bible translations render this as "speaking in tongues." This is not the learning of a language unfamiliar to the speaker. It is a spontaneous speech made possible by the supernatural power of God in a language not known to the speaker.

On the day of Pentecost (Acts 2:6), people around the Jerusalem temple understood the languages the 120 disciples were speaking under the anointing of the Holy Spirit. This, however, does not seem to have been the norm subsequently. First Corinthians 14:2 says that when someone speaks in tongues he or she is speaking to God. In verse 4 of that same chapter, Paul says that "a person who speaks in tongues is strengthened personally."

In this list of nine Holy Spirit gifts, this is the only one that primarily benefits the speaker. Paul goes on to say, "Well then, what shall I do? I will pray in the spirit, and I will also pray in words I understand. I will sing in the spirit, and I will also sing in words I understand" (1 Cor 14:15). Clearly speaking in tongues has a personal role in prayer and worship. In fact, Paul declares to the disciples in Corinth, "I thank God that I speak in tongues more than any of you" (1 Cor 14:18). Speaking in unknown languages, therefore, has a critical role to play in the lives of the individual disciples of Jesus.

THE ABILITY TO INTERPRET WHAT IS BEING SAID

This, like the other eight, is a supernatural gift given by the Holy Spirit to translate, or even paraphrase, a message spoken in a language the interpreter does not know so that the congregation which has heard the message in tongues can understand what has been said.

These nine spiritual gifts are not toys for Christians to play with when assembled. They are critical tools the Church uses for the demonstration of the power of the Holy Spirit in a generation that appears to have rejected Christianity in favor of other ritualistic spiritual observances and now needs to encounter God's power personally.

It must also be noted that these nine gifts of the Holy Spirit can and do overlap in their operation. For example, words of wisdom and knowledge can be delivered within the gift of prophecy. The gifts of faith and miracles can result in remarkably similar outcomes. In the end it is the sovereign demonstration of the gifts by the Holy Spirit that determines their operation and not our human desires and opinions.

Several commentators, in expounding chapters 12 through 14 of the first epistle to the disciples at Corinth, teach that these supernatural gifts given by the Holy Spirit to individual disciples, as he sovereignly determines, are for operation in the Church when assembled in various congregations. It is true that Paul, in this passage of Scripture, gives instructions on how these gifts are to be used in an orderly manner when the Church has assembled. One deduces that times of corporate worship had become confusing and lacking in structure, so that the benefit of these supernatural manifestations in Corinth was being lost to the congregation.

However, even a cursory reading of the book of Acts reveals that these gifts of the Holy Spirit were also used when the disciples were distributed throughout the community at least as much as, if not more than, when they were assembled for corporate worship. Recognizing that the Church in the first century did not have designated buildings for worship as we do today, but used the homes of believers for congregating, we see a situation quite different to that which obtains today in many countries.

This then raises the question of whether the gifts of the Holy Spirit as outlined in these passages, are to be solely confined to our church buildings. A case can be made that the Church distributed through the community needs the demonstration and power of the Holy Spirit as much, if not more than, the Church assembled in its buildings. The apostle Paul seemingly had no hesitation in the use of powerful spiritual gifts outside of the homes where assembled believers met for exhortation, instruction, and fellowship, and even in public spaces.

There is also the issue of pastoral control, a troubling issue in the twenty-first-century church. First Corinthians 12:8–11 places control of these gifts squarely in the hands of the Holy Spirit, not the pastors and other officers of the Church assembled. Leaders within the local church are to teach, edify, and equip the disciples so that they become mature Christians able to function effectively as the Church distributed through the community, not to control those disciples. Regretfully, a small minority of pastors have become so enamored with their personal power that they seek to control and dominate the members of the congregations they lead. This is not of the Holy Spirit and usually constitutes spiritual abuse.

As the Church in the twenty-first century faces unprecedented issues, as well as the resuscitation of some of the sins the first-century Church faced in society, more than ever, the demonstration and power of the Holy Spirit is needed to confirm the gospel that we preach. It is an urgent necessity that disciples of Jesus be equipped with the gifts of the Holy Spirit, taught the Scriptures thoroughly so that they mature spiritually, and are released to take this *dynamis* power to every corner of society. The future of the Church depends on this if Jesus does not return in our lifetimes.

When Jesus sent out his disciples to minister, he instructed them, "Go and announce to them that the kingdom of heaven is near. Heal the sick, raise the dead, cure those with leprosy, and cast out demons. Give as freely as you have received!" (Matt 10:7–8). This principle of giving is in the context of the supernatural. If that principle is applied to contemporary ministry, it suggests that there are supernatural, miraculous gifts to be shared in society by the Church as it ministers in every area of society, where God places his servants.

The exhortation of 1 Thess 5:19 is worth embracing in the twenty-first century, "Do not stifle the Holy Spirit. Do not scoff at prophecies, but test everything that is said. Hold on to what is good. Stay away from every kind of evil."

These remarkable gifts are, essentially, the demonstration of the power of the Holy Spirit through our human vessels and do not represent the totality of the gifts that God has given to the Church. Additional ones are explored in the next chapter. It is important, however, to embrace the principle the apostle Peter lays out, "God has given each of you a gift from his great variety of spiritual gifts. Use them well to serve one another" (1 Pet 4:10). It must be strongly reiterated that these gifts are not for self-aggrandizement or to give individuals power over others. They are given so that we may serve each other.

As the apostle Paul states, "Let love be your highest goal! But you should also desire the special abilities the Spirit gives" (1 Cor 14:1).

Unfortunately, a few people have thought that if the Holy Spirit uses them in one of these remarkable power demonstrations that this somehow entitles them to become a pastor and lead a congregation. Nothing could be further from the truth. God empowers us to function where he places us. Stepping out of that place without God's guidance could be a significant moment of disobedience. In the next chapter we reflect on the grace-gift-persons God gives to the Church.

It is critical that the power gifts of 1 Cor 12 be operated within the character traits of Gal 5. Anything less will cause a dysfunction in life and ministry.

CHAPTER 12

Grace-Gift-Persons

THE MISSION OF THE Church is clearly delineated by Jesus as making disciples (Matt 28:19). In expounding on the Church, the apostle Paul adds this interesting selection of gifts given by Christ to the Church, "Now these are the gifts Christ gave to the church: the apostles, the prophets, the evangelists, and the pastors and teachers" (Eph 4:11).

Given the reality of Peter's spiritual principle that God's gifts are given to us so that we may "serve one another" (1 Pet 4:10), and the principle that Jesus laid down that he did not come to be served but to serve others (Matt 20:28; Mark 10:45), it is spiritually dangerous to turn this list of gifts into a hierarchy within the Church. These gifts are for service above all else, and humility is an essential foundation of service.

Jesus reemphasized this requirement of servanthood over lordship within his kingdom when he said,

> You know that the rulers in this world lord it over their people, and officials flaunt their authority over those under them. But among you it will be different. Whoever wants to be a leader among you must be your servant, and whoever wants to be first among you must become your slave. (Matt 20:25–27)

The apostle Paul is also quite clear about the purpose of these gifts being bestowed on persons selected by Jesus, "Their responsibility is to equip God's people to do his work and build up the church, the body of Christ" (Eph 4:12).

So, how can we understand and utilize these gifts? It is clear from their practical application that the gifts can overlap within one person's ministry and are intended to overlap within team ministry throughout the Church as people.

So, what is this grace-gift-person of apostle?

The Greek word so translated means "someone sent with a message, a representative, someone sent on a specific mission having the authority of the sender." It would seem from the ministry of the apostle Paul, as well as what we know of the ministry of the apostles chosen by Jesus, that these persons had authority, governance, and a role in laying the foundation of the Church in unevangelized territory and setting out the parameters of Christian belief and practice. From the life and ministry of Paul, it seems that apostolic ministry was by no means confined to preaching, but included the discipline and welfare of the Christian community through the oversight of scattered groups of Christians and the operation of the miraculous, grace gifts of power referred to in the last chapter.

The grace-gift-person of apostle seems to have been limited in number from the beginning. In choosing a replacement for Judas in the original twelve, called by Scripture the apostles of the Lamb (Rev 21:14). One qualification was that the person to be chosen had to be one who had been with them the entire time that they had been disciples of Jesus. This clearly sets those twelve people apart as a special select group. This was not, however, intended to limit the grace-gift-person of apostle to only those twelve people in perpetuity.

The acceptance of Paul as an apostle expands the scope of the grace-gift. Paul seems to suggest that Andronicus and Junia were included among those who were apostles, though this verse could be interpreted to mean that the existing apostles highly respected these two persons and not that they were themselves apostles. It seems that Barnabas might also be considered an apostle given his labor alongside Paul and subsequent ground-breaking ministry in spreading the gospel and laying a foundation for others to build on.

Some have taken the position that the grace-gift-person of apostle was limited to the eleven disciples chosen by Jesus and the one added to replace Judas after he committed suicide. However, it seems more logical that the gift of apostle was intended for the Church age. The first twelve apostles will always have a special place in the Church. Yet there is still need for apostolic ministry in taking the Church to people groups who have not heard the gospel, in establishing the boundaries and scope of the faith as new congregations continue to be created, and in the oversight and governance of scattered groups of Christians. There is also the ongoing need for the miraculous in every generation in confronting and defeating the strongholds of the satanic kingdom expressed in various ways across the world. In some ways it is also necessary to build foundations for each generation. The Church is only ever one generation away from apostasy.

Rev. Dennis White, born in Barbados and raised in Trinidad, has had a powerful apostolic ministry. He first went to the Commonwealth of Dominica, where he planted at least five new congregations and laid the foundation for Pentecostal ministry there. He then went over to St. Vincent and the Grenadines and repeated the process. From there he went on to be president of the West Indies School of Theology and, subsequently, general superintendent of the Pentecostal Assemblies of the West Indies. In those roles he built foundations in the lives of young ministers and exercised governance over hundreds of congregations in the eastern Caribbean. White then went to Kenya, where he spent many years planting new assemblies and building up the Church in that country. He has settled in Canada, where he continues to minister in his senior years.

Some denominations have opted to consider their bishops as being in the apostolic succession. Others have postulated that we have superintendents and bishops as we no longer recognize apostolic ministries among us. Given the spiritual and moral realities in the world today, there is a need for apostolic ministry as much as, or more than, any time in the history of the Church.

GRACE-GIFT-PERSONS

These grace-gift-persons also include prophets. There seems to be a range of ways the prophets exercise ministry in the Church. They are the people who encourage, strengthen and comfort others (1 Cor 14:3). Judas and Silas were prophets who encouraged and strengthened the believers in their faith in Antioch (Acts 15:32). There were also the four unmarried daughters of Philip who exercised the gift of prophecy, as did Agabus (Acts 21:8–10).

Prophets can also foretell the future as Agabus did in Acts 11:28 and 21:11. The prophets of the Old Testament understood that God put his words in their mouths for them to speak out (Deut 18:81; Jer 1:9). The same is true of these grace-gift-persons in the New Testament.

In the context of the Church, prophets have a pivotal role in the edification of believers. Never do their words equate to Scripture and never do they contravene the Bible when under the anointing of the Holy Spirit. Any contradictions of Scripture would arise from the human spirit and cannot be equated with the words of the Holy Spirit.

All prophets will exercise the grace-gift of prophecy found in 1 Cor 12:10. However, not everyone who is used by the Holy Spirit in that grace-gift of prophecy rises to the level of the grace-gift-person of prophet to the Church. As with the grace-gift-persons of apostles, prophets were given to the Church for the Church age and are not to be relegated to the first century AD. These gifts are as critical to the life of the Church now as they were when the Church spilled out of Jerusalem and began its journey to the uttermost parts of the earth.

Too much false spirituality is abroad in the world and, sadly, in parts of the Church. Unfortunately, too many people today take to themselves the title of the grace-gift-prophet and mislead many who are undiscerning. Nevertheless, the New Testament prophets of the Church age can and should play a vital role in ensuring the Church remains spiritually strong and focused.

Both apostles and prophets are seen in the New Testament as foundational to the Church. "So now you Gentiles are no longer strangers and foreigners. You are citizens along with all of God's holy people. You are members of God's family. Together, we are his house, built on the foundation of the apostles and the prophets. And the cornerstone is Christ Jesus himself" (Eph 2:19–20). In each generation foundations must, inevitably, be relaid for the Church to be effective, current, and spiritually powerful in order that the Church does not become irrelevant and useless, salt without saltiness and light under a bushel.

The ministry of indigenous apostles and prophets in Africa during the nineteenth and early twentieth centuries was key to bringing a measure of equality between black and white Christians and dividing Christianity from the brutal colonialism that stormed Africa.

The grace-gift-person of evangelist is not mentioned much in Scripture. Indeed, other than Eph 4:11 the term is used only in Acts 21:8 and 2 Tim 4:5 (and in the latter verse some translations do not use the word "evangelist" at all). However, the ministry of an evangelist is certainly alluded to in passages such as Rom 10:14–15. The evangelist in Christian theology is, essentially, the one who proclaims the good news of Jesus Christ that he died and rose again to make salvation available to all who would believe on him.

This grace-gift fortifies, builds, and encourages the Church by adding numerically to local congregations. That this grace-gift is for the entire church age is unquestioned. Down through the centuries there have been many mighty evangelists who have proclaimed the good news of the gospel. One of the foremost such evangelists in the twentieth century was Dr. Billy Graham, while Reinhard Bonnke is another evangelist in the modern era who had a powerful ministry in Africa. There is a plethora of others from every corner of the globe who have proclaimed the good news in their own "heart languages" to their people and nation. The conferences on evangelism held in Amsterdam by the Billy Graham Evangelistic Association were each attended by thousands of evangelists from many cultures and countries across the globe.

An evangelist out of the Caribbean during the twentieth century was the late Rev. Dr. Holmes Williams, from the small island of Barbados. His ministry significantly impacted some countries in the eastern Caribbean, South America, Africa, and elsewhere, and only eternity will show the impact he had in answering God's call to be an evangelist to his generation. Holmes planted what is now known as The People's Cathedral in Barbados and built a congregation of thousands through his gift of evangelism ministry.

The other grace-gift-persons listed in Eph 4:11 are pastor and teacher. These are now often linked together as pastor-teacher since their function is seen to closely overlap and, in several ways, are dependent on each other. Some New Testament scholars are of the view that the grammar of the Greek text strongly suggests the linking of these as two aspects of one gift.

The Greek word for "pastor" is literally translated "shepherd." In biblical times, and even today, the shepherd did not just ensure the flock was properly fed. It was the shepherd's responsibility to tend the sheep, to guide, nourish, apply available medical assistance for the inevitable bruises and cuts, ward against insects like fleas and ticks, and guard against wild animals, such as wolves, bears, and lions, who would kill and eat the sheep. The shepherd's role is quite comprehensive. So too is the role of the pastor.

Each pastor tends the congregation he/she is called to serve, providing holistic care in many different areas of life and spirituality. This person must guard against the ravenous forces of evil that seek to destroy the flock, ward off the predators and insects of sin, and nurture through the emotional, spiritual, and psychological bruises that attack the sheep within his or her fold. The pastor's role, primarily, is one of discipling those brought to Christ by the evangelist.

Teaching is also a key role that a pastor plays within the grace-gift-persons, as outlined in Eph 4. This is very strategic as it connects back to the instructions Jesus gave the disciples/apostles after his resurrection, "Teach these new disciples to obey all the commands I have given you" (Matt 28:20). It is key to the making of true disciples of Jesus, which Matt 28:19 instructs as our most essential task in spiritual leadership.

A particularly important aspect to note is that these four/five grace-gift-persons are given to the Church and their assigned task is specific, as previously noted, "Their responsibility is to equip

Church Is Who We Are

God's people to do his work and build up the church, the body of Christ" (Eph 4:12). Their mandate is to ensure that the Church is effectively trained and spiritually supplied to fulfill its destiny across the landscape of society where God places them to be salt and light. It is, therefore, understandable that, in the current reality, these grace-gift-persons focus on ministry within the buildings where congregations meet. However, they must grasp the reality that the people who they are training and equipping will have a significant part of their own ministry outside of those walls, within society, where the Church is planted.

An interesting leadership team that might be an example of the team leadership God expected to develop through these grace-gift-persons is found in Acts 13:1. The Antioch church had a rich diversity of leadership. This leadership was multi-gifted.

Acts 13:1 tells us, "Among the prophets and teachers at Antioch" were certain individuals. Examine this a little more closely. The team mentioned here was the pastoral leadership team. It is known that Barnabas and Paul were called out and became apostles. The seed of that apostolic ministry must have already been evident. It is also known that Paul had spent three years in evangelism after his conversion and before he went up to Jerusalem. Lucius is probably among those in Acts 11:20, in the role of evangelist, who is thought to have participated in founding the local church in Antioch. So, there were at least two evangelists on the team. Here were budding apostles, recognized prophets, evangelists, and pastors. These grace-gift-persons, bound together by the Holy Spirit, provided leadership to the Antioch church in its initial formative years. It's a model that could be emulated today under the direction of the Holy Spirit.

Notice that not only was the administrative team of the Antioch church multi-gifted but it was also multicultural. Not many of God's people are named in Scripture. The fact that the Holy Spirit names this leadership team is, therefore, of special note.

Barnabas is described, in Acts 11:24, as a "good man, full of the Holy Spirit and strong in faith." His name means son of prophecy, exhortation, and encouragement—the epitome of what is expected of a pastor. He had owned land in Cyprus and was the missionary sent from Jerusalem to pastor the young church at Antioch. He brings in his colleague Paul, a Jew with Roman citizenship, to join the leadership team.

Simeon is called "the black man." It would seem, therefore, that Simeon was a black African. Lucius was from Cyrene, a city in Africa. His name suggests a strong Roman influence, and some have equated him with Luke, who wrote the Gospel of Luke and book of Acts, especially as Cyrene was known for its medical profession.

Manaen was Jewish, but had been brought up among the Roman aristocracy of Herod's household. Manaen probably knew John the Baptist and was quite conceivably present at the party which precipitated John's execution. He would have known Joanna, the wife of Chuza, Herod's steward, who ministered to Jesus. Manaen could well have been present when Jesus stood trial before Herod. He might even have been a boy in Herod the Great's household when the wise men arrived looking for the baby Jesus.

Then there was Paul, the Hebrew of the Hebrews, a Pharisee, of the tribe of Benjamin, the quintessential orthodox Jew (Phil 3:4–6).

God pulls together this culturally diverse group of African, Jew, Roman, physician, landowner, and aristocrat, and fashions a leadership team for the Antioch church. Then, out of that leadership team, he draws the first two great trail blazers of the gospel in Asia Minor and Europe. This gives us a sense of the diversity of the grace-gift-persons in the Church of the first century as it set out to change the world and establish the good news of the gospel for all people.

The Church, as expressed in local congregations throughout society, needs diversity of leadership if it is to become the instrument of change and transformation, as the metaphors of salt and light suggest it should be. These grace-gift-persons are the ones God has given the Church to ensure a sound base, when gathering regularly, to be taught, trained, and equipped for service throughout society.

CHAPTER 13

Powerfully Indwelled

GALATIANS 5:25 SAYS, "SINCE we are living by the Spirit, let us follow the Spirit's leading in every part of our lives." The only way we can truly live out the reality of being Church is to do so with the leading and anointing of the Holy Spirit.

The New Testament book of Ephesians was written while Paul was imprisoned in Rome by Emperor Nero. In many of his letters (epistles) to various groups and individuals, Paul includes a prayer and this is especially so in his prison epistles. Paul's second prayer for the Ephesian Christians is found in the third chapter of that epistle. In the sixteenth verse Paul prays, "I pray that from his glorious, unlimited resources he will empower you with inner strength through his Spirit."

The King James Version translates the start of Paul's prayer as a request that he would "grant" the Holy Spirit to believers. A grant is a gift; there is no request for repayment when a grant is given. It is a timely reminder that we receive freely from God all that he gives because Jesus has already paid the price on the cross. The original Greek version of this verse is very clear about the Holy Spirit being poured into the inside of each believer with the resulting empowerment of spiritual strength expressed in the life of the individual.

If we, indeed, have received from such "unlimited resources," which Swindoll calls a "treasure trove"[1] and Hodge declares to be "everything in God that renders him glorious,"[2] poured into us, we can and should bring those resources to bear in every aspect of our lives. Surely this is part of being salt and light in the communities where we live and work. Such resources cannot be limited to a small percentage of Christian believers operating only in our church buildings at specific times when we gather for worship, fellowship, and edification. It must be available to every Christian in all circumstances wherever we are in the world. It is an ongoing relationship with the indwelling Holy Spirit where we daily receive from God's unlimited resources.

In the next verse in Ephesians, Paul prays that "Christ will make his home in your hearts as you trust in him." The original Greek carries the sense of Jesus feeling at home in our hearts. It is one thing to visit a friend's or family member's home. It is quite another to feel at home and settle down. This is indicative of a very deep relationship between Jesus and believers. It is reminiscent of, and reinforces, his promise, "I am with you always" (Matt 28:20). Boice sees this as Jesus becoming a "permanent resident."[3] As Rom 8:10 says, "Christ lives within you." This indwelling is holistic, entering every area of life spiritually, emotionally, intellectually, and physically. This is activated by trust and faith in God's grace as we humans are finite and fallible, making us unworthy of, and incapable of, earning such an incredible life reality.

When someone moves into a house, they usually make changes to turn the house into a home. Walls may be repainted, curtains or drapes hung, carefully chosen art placed, etc. These things all help us to settle down and feel at home. Similarly, when we receive Christ, or are received by Christ, he will do some heart refurbishing and renovating so that he may settle down and feel at home within us.

---

1. Swindoll, *Galatians, Ephesians*, 221.
2. Hodge, *Ephesians*, 181.
3. Boice, *Ephesians*, 110.

Church Is Who We Are

In the nineteenth verse, Paul prays that the Ephesians would experience "the love of Christ, though it is too great to understand fully." The Greek word Paul used here for "love" is *agape*, which the apostle defines extensively in 1 Cor 13, and has been described by many Christian commentators as the highest form of love known to us humans. Experiencing such love is as transformative as receiving the empowering "inner strength" of the Holy Spirit. Living in this love on a day-to-day basis changes our own lives and brings change to every situation we are in, whether at home, at work, at school, at church, or out and about in the community where we live.

In the original Greek the apostle uses a mixed metaphor, speaking in some English translations of being "rooted" (an agricultural term) and "grounded" (an architectural term). Both metaphors are appropriate in expressing a relationship that continually grows stronger. Being rooted in love demonstrates the nurture and sustenance that comes from going deep into God's unfathomable love and producing the fruit that naturally grows from that rooted connection. Being grounded denotes the very firm foundation that God's love provides for building one's life and pursuing one's purpose. It provides a solid underpinning that can withstand the storms of life.

When the apostle speaks of the width, depth, height, and length of God's love, he is expressing the infinite qualities of that love. We may never fully understand such love, but we can experience it daily in our walk with Jesus.

The next request of Paul in this prayer is that the believers in Ephesus would be "made complete with all the fullness of life and power that comes from God" (Eph 3:19). Such a fullness of life is almost beyond our comprehension. Imagine every Christian at every level of society being the Church and expressing this "fullness of life and power" wherever they are and in whatever they do. This is a third transformative reality, inevitable personal and societal transformation.

Here Paul envisages finite humans being able to access the infiniteness of God so that they become complete, whole. God intends this to be part of our daily experience as we journey with him through life and not just a one-off experience in the church building on Sunday mornings.

Paul's prayer then climaxes "Now all glory to God, who is able, through his mighty power at work within us, to accomplish infinitely more than we might ask or think. Glory to him in the church and in Christ Jesus through all generations forever and ever! Amen" (Eph 3:20–21). What an astounding reality!

God can accomplish infinitely more than we can even think through his mighty power within us—the resources of the Holy Spirit poured into us, the incomprehensible love of Jesus as our foundation and source of nurture, Jesus settling down and being at home within us, and the infinite fullness of God's life and power making us complete. Through this means, God's glory is demonstrated through the Church in all generations, even in the twenty-first century, where Western society seems to be ever more impervious to the gospel of Jesus Christ and rapidly shifting away from biblical norms.

The epistles Paul wrote while imprisoned in Rome have an identical format. The first half of the epistle sets out astounding theological truths. The second half shows a practical application of those truths. Ephesians 3:16–21 is placed in a pivotal position between theological doctrines and practical applications in the book of Ephesians. The indwelling presence of the Father, Son, and Holy Spirit provides the spiritual power to transform powerful doctrines into strong life experiences. This realization enables us to be the salt, light, and yeast wherever we are located. As finite human beings we are incapable of doing this on our own. We do not have to. God has provided an infilling of the Trinity to give us the spiritual resources to live out our purpose in each generation.

It is important to stress that the glory all belongs to God. God does not bless us with such inner power in order that we aggrandize ourselves and become great in the eyes of others. It is that he may be glorified through us. When we try to hang on to the glory for ourselves, we begin to deny the reality of God and inevitably bring ourselves into disrepute. Take this seriously.

Epilogue

As these words are being penned the drums of war seem to be sounding across the world. Nations that have not experienced war since 1945 are discussing building up their military forces and ensuring they are properly equipped to be an effective fighting power in the third decade of the twenty-first century. Among the cascading effects being felt globally are an increasing cost of living and shortages brought on by supply chain challenges.

The Church in the West, which has, for centuries, worshiped in complete freedom, is now dealing with restrictions it never previously thought possible. Increasingly, national cultures, previously considered Christian, are becoming impervious to Christian teaching, mores, and values. In many ways it feels like Western societies are being reset to the pre-Christian norms of two millennia ago.

Through widespread immigration, non-Christian forms of spirituality are spreading across the West. Increasingly, the Church is being pushed to not just be ecumenical but to engage in interfaith cooperation and worship.

Yet, we who are the Church must understand our unique position within society and the imperative given us by Jesus to shine as lights, flavor like salt, and spread yeast throughout the culture in which we live. There really can be no holding back, especially as so many Christian leaders believe we are rapidly approaching the return of Jesus as the Conquering Lion and King of kings.

Yes, we are surrounded by increasing sinfulness and rejection of our gospel message. Isaiah 59 paints a picture of a wicked, disobedient, and rebellious society. Yet the prophet declared, "He will come like a raging flood tide driven by the breath of the Lord" (Isa 59:19). Are we living in such a moment?

These are interesting and exciting days, even though sometimes a bit scary. This is the moment for the Church, the people who know their God and who they are, to shake off the complacency and inertia that are partly the result of the COVID-19 pandemic lockdowns, and realize and live out their spiritual reality.

To strengthen that reality, time needs to be spent daily in God's presence worshiping, praying, and studying the Scriptures. There is no shortcut. We neglect this to our peril. Life seems to be busier than ever and getting even busier. Yet we cannot abandon our spiritual health or even move it downwards in our priorities. To do so is to become ineffective as salt and light in the societies where we live and work. There must not be a continuing disconnect between what is celebrated on Sunday and what is practiced the rest of the week. It is said of John Wesley that he prayed for one hour every day except when he had a very busy day, when he prayed for two hours.

This book has been written as an urgent call for the Church to be the transformative instrument of God in our world at every level of society.

Let us *be* the Church wherever God has placed us.

Bibliography

Akin, Daniel L., ed. *A Theology for the Christian Church*. Nashville: B & H, 2007.
Anonymous. Editorial. *Midweek Nation*, Aug. 18, 2020.
Arnold, Clinton E., ed. *Zondervan Illustrated Bible Background Commentary*. 4 vols. Grand Rapids: Zondervan, 2002.
Arnold, Johnathan. "St. Patrick's Day Belongs to the Church: Remembering Ireland's Missionary." *Holy Joys*. Mar. 16, 2022. https://holyjoys.org/patrick-church-ireland/.
Barna, George. *The Power of Vision*. Ventura, CA: Regal, 2003.
Berkhof, Louis. *Systematic Theology*. Grand Rapids: Eerdmans, 1941.
Blomberg, Craig. *1 Corinthians*. NIV Application Commentary. Grand Rapids: Zondervan, 1994.
Boice, James Montgomery. *Ephesians: An Expositional Commentary*. Grand Rapids: Baker, 2003.
———. *Romans: An Expositional Commentary*. Grand Rapids: Baker, 1995.
Brown, Colin, ed. *The New International Dictionary of New Testament Theology*. Grand Rapids: Zondervan, 1975.
Bruce, F. F. *The Gospel and Epistles of John*. Grand Rapids: Eerdmans, 1983.
Bullinger, Ethelbert W. *A Critical Lexicon and Concordance to the English and Greek New Testament*. London: Bagster, 1908.
Cahn, Jonathon. *The Return of the Gods*. Lake Mary, FL: Frontline, 2022.
Carter, Henderson. *Moulding Communities, Touching Lives: A History of the Church of the Nazarene in Barbados 1926–2008*. Kingston, Jamaica: Randle, 2008.
Chafer, Lewis Sperry. *Systematic Theology*. 7 vols. Dallas: Dallas Seminary Press, 1980.
Colson, Charles, and Nancy Pearcy. *How Now Shall We Live?* Wheaton, IL: Tyndale, 1999.
Comissiong, David. *Spiritual Guidance for the Caribbean Church and Its People: Rev. Vivian Comissiong, Methodist Minister*. Bridgetown, Barbados: Self-published, 2020.
Cunningham, Loren. *The Book That Transforms Nations*. Singapore: YWAM Singapore, 2006.

BIBLIOGRAPHY

Dusing, Michael L. "The New Testament Church." In *Systematic Theology*, edited by Stanley M. Horton, 525–66. Rev. ed. Springfield, MO: Logion, 2007.

Edwards, Joel. *An Agenda for Change*. Grand Rapids: Zondervan, 2008.

Erickson, Millard J. *Christian Theology*. Manila, Philippines: Christian Growth Ministry, 1997.

Guthrie, Donald. *New Testament Theology*. Secunderabad, India: OM, 2005.

Guthrie, George H. *Hebrews*. NIV Application Commentary. Grand Rapids: Zondervan, 1998.

Hafemann, Scott J. *2 Corinthians*. NIV Application Commentary. Grand Rapids: Zondervan, 2000.

Halcomb, James, et al. *Courageous Leaders Transforming Their World*. Seattle: YWAM, 2000.

Handschumacher, William. "The Stanley Covenant." Rock of Offense. Accessed Aug. 16, 2024. https://www.rockofoffence.com/myst5.html.

Harrison, Everett F., ed. *Baker's Dictionary of Theology*. Grand Rapids: Baker, 1981.

Hillman, Os. *Faith and Work: Do They Mix?* Cumming, GA: Aslan, 2000.

Hodge, Charles. *Commentary on the Epistle to the Ephesians*. Grand Rapids: Eerdmans, 1857.

Horton, Stanley M. *First and Second Corinthians*. Springfield, MO: Gospel, 1999.

———, ed. *Systematic Theology*. Rev. ed. Springfield, MO: Logion, 2007.

Humes, James C. *The Wit and Wisdom of Winston Churchill*. New York: HarperCollins, 1994.

Jukes, Andrew. *The Law of the Offerings*. 17th ed. Grand Rapids: Kregel, 1854.

Kinnaman, David, and Mark Matlock. *Faith for Exiles*. Grand Rapids: Baker, 2019.

Larkin, William J., Jr. *Acts*. Leicester, England: Inter-Varsity, 1995.

Lewis, Robert. *The Church of Irresistible Influence*. Grand Rapids: Zondervan, 2001.

Maura, Michael Otieno, et al. *Prosperity? Seeking the True Gospel*. Nairobi, Kenya: Africa Christian, 2015.

McKnight, Scott. *1 Peter*. NIV Application Commentary. Grand Rapids: Zondervan, 1996.

———. *Galatians*. NIV Application Commentary. Grand Rapids: Zondervan, 1995.

Menzies, William, and Stanley M. Horton. *Bible Doctrines: A Pentecostal Perspective*. Springfield, MO: Logion, 2015.

Merrill, Eugene H. *Kingdom of Priests: A History of Old Testament Israel*. Grand Rapids: Baker Academic, 1996.

Miller, Calvin. *The Empowered Leader: 10 Keys to Servant Leadership*. Nashville: Broadman & Holman, 1995.

Miller, Kevin A. "Why Did Columbus Sail?" *Christian History*, 1992. https://christianhistoryinstitute.org/magazine/article/why-did-columbus-sail.

BIBLIOGRAPHY

Moo, J. Douglas. *Romans*. NIV Application Commentary. Grand Rapids: Zondervan, 2000.

Morris, Henry M. *The Genesis Record*. Grand Rapids: Baker, 1977.

Munroe, Myles. *God's Big Idea*. Shippensburg, PA: Destiny Image, 2008.

Naisbitt, John. *Mind Set! Reset Your Thinking and See the Future*. New York: HarperCollins, 2006.

Nash, Laura, and Scotty McLennan. *Church on Sunday, Work on Monday*. San Francisco: Jossey-Bass, 2001.

Naugle, David K. *Worldview: The History of a Concept*. Grand Rapids: Eerdmans, 2002.

Okorocha, Cyril. "Psalms." In *Africa Bible Commentary*, edited by Tokunboh Adeyemo, 605–746. Nairobi, Kenya: Word Alive, 2006.

Pakenham, Thomas. *The Scramble for Africa: White Man's Conquest of the Dark Continent from 1876 to 1912*. New York: HarperCollins, 2003.

Prince, Derek. *The Gifts of the Spirit*. New Kensington, PA: Whitaker, 2007.

Purcell, Joan. *Memoirs of a Woman in Politics: Spiritual Struggles*. Bloomington, IN: Authorhouse, 2009.

Rabey, Steve, and Lois Rabey, eds. *Side by Side: A Handbook*. Colorado Springs: Cook Communication Ministries, 2000.

Robinson, Anthony B., and Robert Wall. *Called to Be Church: The Book of Acts for a New Day*. Grand Rapids: Eerdmans, 2006.

Robinson, William Childs. "Church." In *Baker's Dictionary of Theology*, edited by Everett F. Harrison, 123–27. Grand Rapids: Baker, 1960.

Robison, James. *The Absolutes*. Wheaton, IL: Tyndale, 2002.

Ryrie, Charles C. *Basic Theology*. Chicago: Moody, 1999.

Sauder, Brian. *A Practical Path to a Prosperous Life*. Litiz, PA: House to House, 2013.

Shaw, Mark. "A Hunger for Holiness." *Christian History*, 2003. https://christianhistoryinstitute.org/magazine/article/hunger-for-holiness.

Sherlock, Philip, and Hazel Bennett. *The Story of the Jamaican People*. Kingston, Jamaica: Randle, 1998.

Sire, James W. *Naming the Elephant: Worldview as a Concept*. Downers Grove, IL: InterVarsity, 2004.

Snodgrass, Klyne. *Ephesians*. NIV Application Commentary. Grand Rapids: Zondervan, 1996.

Soungalo, Soro. "The Family and Community." In *Africa Bible Commentary*, edited by Tokunboh Adeyemo, 1178. Nairobi, Kenya: Word Alive, 2006.

Spangler, Ann, and Lois Tverberg. *Sitting at the Feet of Rabbi Jesus: How the Jewishness of Jesus Can Transform Your Faith*. Grand Rapids: Zondervan, 2009.

Stanley, Andy. *Not in It to Win It*. Grand Rapids: Zondervan, 2022.

Stott, John R. W. *The Message of Acts: The Spirit, the World, and the Church*. Leicester, England: Inter-Varsity, 1990.

Swindoll, Charles. *Galatians, Ephesians*. Living Insights New Testament Commentary. Carol Stream, IL: Tyndale, 2015.

BIBLIOGRAPHY

―――. *Insights on Acts*. Carol Stream, IL: Tyndale, 2016.
Telushkin, Joseph. *The Book of Jewish Values*. New York: Bell Tower, 2000.
―――. *Jewish Wisdom: Ethical, Spiritual, and Historical Lessons from the Great Works and Thinkers*. New York: Morrow, 1994.
Thielman, Frank. *Philippians*. NIV Application Commentary. Grand Rapids: Zondervan, 1995.
Thiessen, Henry C. *Lectures in Systematic Theology*. Grand Rapids: Eerdmans, 1983.
Tranter, Nigel. *David the Prince*. Sevenoaks, England: Hodder and Stoughton, 1982.
―――. *The Story of Scotland*. Glasgow: Wilson, 2005.
Wanak, Lee, ed. *The Church and Poverty in Asia*. Manila, Philippines: OMF, 2008.
Wiersbe, Warren. *Bible Exposition Commentary: New Testament*. 2 vols. Colorado Springs: Cook Communications Ministries, 2001.
Wilkins, Michael J. *Matthew*. NIV Application Commentary. Grand Rapids: Zondervan, 2004.
Winter, Bruce W. *Seek the Welfare of the City: Christians as Benefactors and Citizens*. Grand Rapids: Eerdmans, 1994.
Wonsuk, Ma. "Jesus Christ in Asia: Our Journey with Him as Pentecostal Believers." Paper presented at the Global Christian Forum Asia Consultation, Hong Kong, 2004.
Wuest, Kenneth S. *Wuest's Word Studies from the Greek New Testament for the English Reader*. 3 vols. Grand Rapids: Eerdmans, 2019.
Youseff, Michael. *The Leadership Style of Jesus*. Wheaton, IL: Victor, 1986.

www.ingramcontent.com/pod-product-compliance
Lightning Source LLC
Chambersburg PA
CBHW070458090426
42735CB00012B/2602